D1109897

complete guide to organizing and documenting research papers

ABOUT THE AUTHOR

Grant W. Morse received his B. A. at Ottawa University, Kansas, his M. S. in Library Science at the State University of New York at Albany, and a M. Div. from E. B. T. S., Philadephia, Pa.

Mr. Morse is a member of the American Association of University Professors and of the Association of University of Wisconsin Faculties. He has been Assistant Librarian at Carthage College and Head Librarian at Findlay College, Ottawa University, Grove City College, Wagner College, and since 1966, at the University of Wisconsin Center-Barron County, Rice Lake, Wisconsin. Mr. Morse has also authored: The Concise Guide to Library Research, *1966 and* Filing Rules for a Three-Way Divided Card Catalog, *1971.*

complete guide to organizing and documenting research papers

by GRANT W. MORSE

Head Librarian,
University of Wisconsin Center
Barron County, Rice Lake, Wisconsin

FLEET ACADEMIC EDITIONS, INC.
New York

DEDICATION

To my wife, Jocelyn

ACKNOWLEDGMENTS

I would like to thank those who have offered many helpful suggestions, especially Dr. Eugene W. Etheridge for his extensive comments.

160 Fifth Avenue
New York, N.Y. 10010

Library of Congress Catalogue Card No.: 73-83969
SBN 8303-0129-1

MANUFACTURED IN THE UNITED STATES OF AMERICA

foreword

It has been my experience during twelve consecutive years of teaching Freshman English that materials on writing the research paper are usually unsatisfactory. I say this for two reasons: either the student must rely on the scanty treatment occuring as a chapter in his assigned grammar, or he may be required to purchase a prolix, book-length treatment more appropiate for graduate students. A few years ago, I started wondering why someone didn't prepare a term paper handbook especially for freshman. It is gratifying to see a few of such texts now on the market, the best of which, in my opinion, is THE COMPLETE GUIDE TO ORGANIZING AND DOCUMENTING RESEARCH PAPERS, by Grant Morse, an expert on the subject.

This handy book has many things going for it. It is throughly and conspicuously indexed, so the student will not have to wander through an acre to find an inch. Each item is clearly illustrated by an example—one that appears exactly as it would look in a term paper. In organizing his material, Mr. Morse is to be commended for separating the background process from the specifics of format. The student who already knows the former but is a bit hazy about the latter will find such a division helpful. Finally, Mr. Morse has struck a balance between brevity and clarity; he is neither verbose and prolix, on the one hand, nor incomplete on the other.

I don't suppose anyone will ever write a text on this subject that "reads like a novel," but Grant Morse has, in my judgment, done the best possible job. His explanations are always clear and brief as possible. I am certain this guide will prove a comforting companion to students, most of whom do not have a paper to write but, sadly enough, have to write a paper.

DR. EUGENE W. ETHERIDGE
Associate Professor of English
Indiana State University

Introduction

A student will not be in college long before he is bombarded with more "research" papers than he can scarcely imagine. Although the "mechanics" of a paper may never excite him, the bibliography, citing sources, and so forth, can be made "compatible." This guide assumes that at least a tentative topic has been chosen and narrowed sufficiently to get started.

In general, the purpose of a typical research paper in college is to require a student to demonstrate his ability to select from various sources, extracting those facts and ideas pertinent to his topic, and interpreting and organizing them into a coherent paper. This involves expressing ideas clearly and effectively, as well as another person's ideas clearly and correctly. In addition, the aim is to help the student judge the reliability and usefulness of sources.

The mechanics of documentation, as a student views it, is that part of a research paper which causes the greatest confusion, consumes excessive time, brings down the wrath of a professor over "trifles," yet counts little toward a good grade. However, documentation is one of the neccesary educational evils which a student must endure when he writes a research paper. The attempt here is to make the mechanics of documentation as clear as possible, as comprehensive as practical, and as consistent in form for all sources used as is attainable. Therefore, brief citing of sources and a simplified bibliography is introduced.

What are the possible methods of organizing your materials? How do you document sources? How do you record your research? Do you have problems with footnotes? Does the bibliography format become a tedious or exasperating experience when you attempt to list your sources? I hope to show the inexperienced college student as well as the graduate student procedures which will aid him in translating his research into a paper.

The method of citing notes at the foot of the page as used in this guide avoids the complexities encountered in other documentation guides. Likewise, the bibliography style of entry is both simplified and provides that all types of source materials (books, periodicals, letters, manuscripts, and so forth) conform to the same basic order. Only brief familiarity with this method of documenting provides you with the solution to citing and listing virtually every source, even those sources which would normally be found difficult by other methods. Although extended details and examples of citation notes and bibliography entries are given here, they will seldom need to be consulted. This guide emphasizes comprehensiveness of treatment for students rather than as some guides, seeming to sacrifice clarity for brevity. The flexibility of this guide makes it as useful to the beginning researcher as for the graduate student, selecting only those sections which are applicable.

The subject matter is divided into five main sections for the convenience of the user. This enables the researcher to focus on or exclude materials not needed. The general topic of typing, format, and expression are reviewed in the first section. This basic information is applicable to all papers. The section on "Organization of Materials" is primarily intended for the beginning research student although useful to even the graduate researcher. The next three sections focus on the paper itself: "Preliminary Pages," the "Text" and its use of sources, followed by the "Supplementary Pages" which includes the bibliography format. A helpful appendix with an extensive index conclude the guide.

Simplicity, efficiency, uniformity, and comprehensiveness characterize the organization of this book.

Contents

General Mechanics of a Paper

TYPING AND GENERAL FORMAT

Neatness and clarity of format, the general physical appearance of the paper, set the proper mode for the reader. He will be impressed, and we hope favorably, by the general appearance of the manuscript long before he will be impressed by the contents. The preferences of the department concerned should be observed with any paper. The following information is applicable to both writer and typist and will aid in producing a satisfactory finished paper.

Although the typist is responsible for an accurate, neat, and generally good appearance of the final copy, the writer is fully responsible for the paper's correctness of content, references, illustrative materials, and editing. The typist is held responsible only for the mechanical details. Suggestions for the typist follow:

Typewriter—Unless permission is granted ahead of time, use a standard or electric typewriter with either pica (preferred) or elite type Keep the type and roller clean. A plain type face, rather than unusual style, is preferred.

Ribbon—if a carbon-paper ribbon is not available for your model of typewriter, use a medium-inked ribbon. Use the ribbon a short while before typing the actual paper. In order to maintain a uniform shade of type the supply of ribbon should be sufficient so as to allow ribbon changes every twenty-five pages.

Paper—Use a high quality bond paper of twenty-pound weight, 8½ x 11 inches in size. Lighter weight paper may be used for carbon copies. To insure that all pages of a given copy are of identical color, weight, and texture buy an adequate supply of paper before starting. Use only one side.

Additional copies—A first-rate copy machine will reproduce clearer copies than carbon paper and will not smudge. Make at least one carbon copy of each revision, however, and keep these in a separate place for safekeeping. Use new carbon after every four or five typed pages for sharp and clear copies.

Spacing—Use double-spacing except for lengthy quotations, content notes, and the bibliography which are single-spaced. Double space between items which are single-spaced. See additional information under special topics, e.g., title page, bibliography, etc.

Making corrections—Corrections should be few and be neat. Do not strike over or cross out words or letters—either erase and retype or retype the entire page. Never use pen or pencil corrections. Do not crowd two letters together in the space meant for one. Proofreading and correcting copies after every ten pages of typing will lessen the difference between the blackness of the original copy and the correct copy. If in doubt as to the final appearance of the paper, retype it.

Page numbers—Do not type page numbers until the paper is finished and proofread. To maintain order in the paper, number each page lightly in pencil as the pages are typed. Count every page, even though a number may not be shown, e.g., on title page. Preliminary pages are numbered with small Roman numerals (i, ii, iii, iv) at the bottom of all pages, centered. The only exception involves each page with a major heading, where the number is centered at the foot of the page, about six spaces (1¼″) from the bottom of the page.

Indention—The first line of a paragraph of the text and the entire quoted material are indented the same distance (five spaces) from the left margin.

Margins—If there is room for only one line of a new paragraph at the bottom of the page, begin the paragraph on next page. See the facsimile pages.

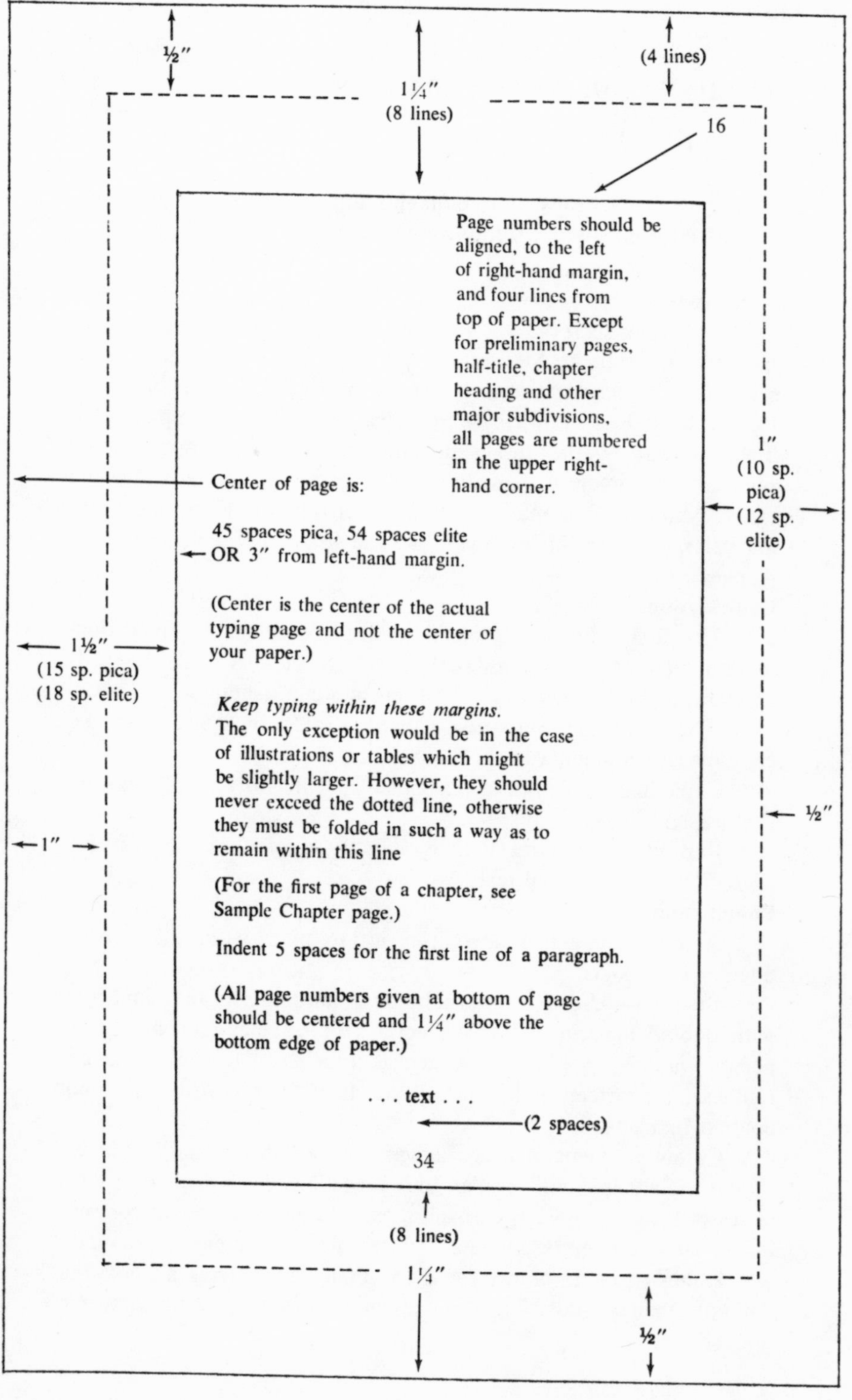
½″
1¼″
(8 lines)
(4 lines)
16
Page numbers should be aligned, to the left of right-hand margin, and four lines from top of paper. Except for preliminary pages, half-title, chapter heading and other major subdivisions, all pages are numbered in the upper right-hand corner.
Center of page is:
45 spaces pica, 54 spaces elite OR 3″ from left-hand margin.
(Center is the center of the actual typing page and not the center of your paper.)
1″
(10 sp. pica)
(12 sp. elite)
1½″
(15 sp. pica)
(18 sp. elite)
Keep typing within these margins.
The only exception would be in the case of illustrations or tables which might be slightly larger. However, they should never exceed the dotted line, otherwise they must be folded in such a way as to remain within this line
(For the first page of a chapter, see Sample Chapter page.)
Indent 5 spaces for the first line of a paragraph.
(All page numbers given at bottom of page should be centered and 1¼″ above the bottom edge of paper.)
½″
1″
. . . text . . .
(2 spaces)
34
(8 lines)
1¼″
½″

MECHANICS OF EXPRESSION

These suggestions and comments are for reminding the writer of frequently misused writing practices.

Abbreviations

As a rule, spell out all words in the text rather than abbreviate. Exceptions would be Mr., Mrs., Dr., Rev., some mathematical and scientific formulas, and so forth. When an organization or broadcasting station is best known by its initials, spell out the complete name first, followed by the initials in parentheses. If the organization is referred to frequently thereafter in the paper, the initials are sufficient. Abbreviations may be used effectively in notes, illustrative materials, and the bibliography. See the list of abbreviations in the Appendix.

Capitalization

The first letters of principal words of titles of publications, motion pictures, recordings, table headings, and so forth should be capitalized. Full capitals may be used in some headings.

When referring to a specific chapter, table, or figure in the text, capitalize the first letter of each, e.g., Table 8.

Capitalize references to parts of a specific work, e.g., Johnson's Preface and Index.

Reproduce material that is directly quoted exactly as it is presented in the original text.

Punctuation

A few comments follow in regard to punctuation that are frequently overlooked.

Brackets—Use for interpolations, particularly in connection with quoted materials. Any corrections or original remarks by the person quoting should be inserted in brackets [ ]. Never use parentheses ( ) instead of brackets. Use ink if the typewriter does not contain brackets.

Commas—General usage leaves optional the choice of placing a comma before "and" or the "or" preceding the last element of a series of three or more words, phrases, or clauses. Place all commas inside quotation marks, unless a parenthetical reference intervenes.

Colon—Use a colon (:) when formally introducing a quotation but not when a quotation is an integral element of your sentence.

Dashes—A dash is typed as two unspaced hyphens. No space should precede or follow the dash (--).

Defining words—A term should be enclosed in quotation marks when being defined. Subsequent use of the same term is made without quotation marks.

Ditto marks—Never use ditto marks in a formal paper except when they are in quoted material.

Ellipsis marks—If needed, omit nonessential material from a quotation with an ellipsis mark consisting of three . . . spaced dots (periods), a space before each dot and after the last dot. The three dots will always be in addition to any period (or other punctuation) marking the end of a sentence. Ellipsis marks are always placed inside quotation marks.

Examples:

Omission within a quote:

"so great . . . distance between God and the creature."

Punctuation immediately before or after the omission is included in the quote:

"In the case of our human friends we take their existence for granted, not caring whether it is proved or not. . . . I think that it is something of the same kind of security we should seek in our relationship with God."

". . . ; while to those, if such existed, with whom God has had no such dealings, argument would be as little use as it would be to those, . . . , who had never met a fellow man."

". . . argument, in spite of all we have said against a certain use of it, has a true office to perform with respect to the divine existence, . . ."

Omission of one or more paragraphs within a quote separated from the text is shown by typing only the ellipsis mark on a separate line, followed on the next line by repeating the ellipsis mark and the quoted material:

"Choose a topic that you can handle in the time and word length allotted for the paper. . . .

. . .

. . . topics may be found by glancing through the card catalog, encyclopedias, dictionaries, and the like."

When the omission is both lengthy and within the text, it is shown by six spaced periods, i.e., a space before each period and after the last:

"Is the work reliable . . . . . . Is the material up-to-date? . . ."

Enumerated materials—As to enumeration of items, when they are brief and woven into the text, the figures or letter should be enclosed in parentheses, i.e., (1), (2) with no punctuation marks following the parentheses.

A good bibliography meets these qualifications: (1) completeness of your source, (2) uniformity of sequence, (3) and enough flexibility to make possible the inclusion of complex information in a consistent manner.

For items that are part of a sentence or already numbered, enumerate the item with lower-case letters in parentheses. Lengthy items without subdivisions are indented (5 spaces) from the left margin in tabular form:

1.
2.
3.

The first word of each item in the above list should be capitalized. See further information on enumeration under the discussion of the table of contents, illustrative materials, and outlines.

Exclamation marks—Avoid using exclamation marks in scholarly writing.

Foreign words, phrases, and letters—When these are used, English translations of such should be in quotation marks. In linguistic studies, foreign words, phrases, and letters are to be underlined and single quotation marks used for definitions or translations.

Hyphens—Avoid ending a line with a hyphen. If in doubt as to the correct place to divide a word, consult a dictionary.

Interpolations—Interpolations of your own within quoted material is permissible if enclosed in square [] brackets (never parentheses). If your typewriter has no brackets, interpolations may be inserted into the paper by hand in black ink. The word *sic* (meaning "so" and underlined) may be placed immediately after an error, i.e., [sic] within the quotation itself. This may be used to assure the reader of the exactness of the quotation, or you may wish to supply a correction and/or add a brief comment.

Italics or underlining—Underlining is the typist's method of italicizing, and unless you can change the type style of the typewriter being used, underscore all words italicized. Underline each word separately.

1. Italic style of print is used for emphasis.

2. The underscoring may be used to indicate proper rendering of a quotation.

3. If you wish to emphasize certain words in a quotation, you may underscore and either immediately follow in square brackets [italics mine] or make a parenthetical note following the quotation and quotation marks (Italics mine) or put in the foot note the fact that the italic is yours.

4. The major titles of a book or periodical are underlined whenever they appear. Some prefer typing a major title in all capitals (ask your advisor). Titles occurring within a book or periodical are enclosed in quotation marks.

5. Although foreign words are usually underlined, consult your advisor about the most acceptable rules of underlining in your institution.

Periods—Do not use periods in titles, the table of contents, or following the heading (other than paragraph sideheadings). Place all periods inside quotation marks unless a parenthetical reference intervenes. Other punctuation goes outside quotation marks unless they are actually part of the passage quoted.

Quotation marks—Enclose the passage with double quotation marks. When double quotation marks occur within the passage you are quoting, they must be changed to single quotation marks. Alternate double and single quotation marks for yet another quotation within, and so on. Place all periods and commas inside quotation marks unless a parenthetical reference intervenes. Other punctuation goes outside quotation marks unless they are actually part of the passage quoted. When the quotation is single-spaced, indented five spaces from the left margin, and separated from the text, omit the marks at the beginning and the end. Use quotation marks when a short passage is being quoted within the text. Examples are given below in relation to the citation note reference:

1. When the quotation is part of your text, place the footnote number reference (Citation Note) *after* the quotation marks. ". . . to qualify as a missing link."[1]

2. When the quotation is *separated from the text,* place the footnote number *after all* punctuation marks. . . . of their adaptations and specializations.[2]

3. Type with single spacing all of the quotations not included in the text.

See further information on quotations under Ellipsis marks above and Recording the Findings.

Word divisions—Avoid dividing words at the end of a line. Do not divide and run over to a second line dates, hours of the day, figures of any type, or the name of the month and the day. Any doubts as to approved word-divisions should be checked in a dictionary.

Spelling

When in doubt, look up the word in a good dictionary. Reproduce material that is directly quoted exactly as it appears in the original text. Be consistent in spelling when a word may be correctly spelled in more than one way. Also see information under capitalization and abbreviations.

Organization of Material

THE APPROACH

An organized beginning makes for an economy of time and means. Haphazard jumping here and there can be a most frustrating experience as well as a great waste of time. Some students will unconsciously approach their research from a general organizational viewpoint. Whether this is an unconscious or a conscious organizational approach, he will tend to follow one of the four basic methods discussed below: The Unfolding Method, The Applied Method, The Experimental Method, and The Theoretical Method. Although all of these organizational methods may be introduced into a given research paper, one method will always predominate. These four basic methods are like four separate spotlights shining on the same general area: each light will be distinctive, yet overlap the others.

The discussion on organizational approach is introduced here primarily for its effect on, and its usefulness in, note-taking and outlining. The four methods are arranged progressively in order of increasing difficulty to master. First, The Unfolding or Inductive Method is usually the choice of the inexperienced researcher, as it confines his research primarily to books and documents. Second, The Applied Method emphasizes a practical application. Third, The Experimental Method implies tentative acceptance of a premise, control and a final or summarizing conclusion. Fourth is The Theoretical Method, terminating in theory or speculation. The Theoretical is usually found to be of greater difficulty for the undergraduate.

The Unfolding Method

This method may be helpful not only in historical areas or subjects but also in those areas which are not confined to chronology. For the historical point of view, one focuses on one of the following:

Development

Stresses the drawing out of hidden or latent possibilities in a concrete object or an idea. It implies growth through a series of natural stages.

Evolution

Stresses an orderly succession of events, things, or ideas, each growing out of that which precedes it, giving it a more complex and different character, yet retaining a likeness to the original.

Chronological

Pertains more to the order of time in past events.

This unfolding is more than just historical; it is also a revealing or disclosing or meaning not confined to time, such as with poetry or prose. It may be to interpret, expand, explain, or compare a passage or subject. Taking questionnaires, interviewing, or inspecting may be involved in this type of unfolding.

Here, the material tends to dictate the initial organization, a logical outgrowth of one's emphasis. If the emphasis is on the historical, we would have an outline somewhat as follows:

I. Starting Point or Thesis
II. Successive or Consecutive Steps (a time concept)
III. Conclusion

A basic outline emphasizing that aspect of the unfolding method not confined to "time" is much the same as above—with one exception, Step II, "Successive or Consecutive." ("Successive or Consecutive" implies steps which follow one another without interruption. Successive suggests variance in the regularity of these steps, while consecutive stresses regularity or order.) We thus have the following difference in basic outlines:

I. Starting Point or Thesis
II. Disclosure
III. Conclusion

The disclosure is the opening up of the idea or subject by expanding, interpreting, explaining, or comparing the passage rather than by a continuous line of "time" order.

Suggested sample subjects and titles:

Notes on the Evolution of German Renaissance Lyricism
Problem of a Religious Interpretation of Gulliver's Fourth Voyage
Literature in its Relation to Norwegian-American History
Date and Evolution of Edmund Volton's Hypercritica
The New Morality
Social Change
Conflict and Criminality
Recent Developments in Heart Surgery

The Applied Method

This method treats a subject by making a connection or bringing it into contact for a practical application. It is opposed to the purely theoretical. It involves clarification of a problem. The direction is toward arriving at the "best," the most advantageous, the most worthwhile, the most useful or valuable solution. A survey would be one example of this method. This method would outline as follows:

I. Ascertain the Facts
II. Weigh the Facts
III. Propose Solutions
IV. Select a Solution, A Conclusion, or Both
V. Suggest a Means for Achieving Part IV

Ascertain the Facts

This assumes objectivity on the part of the researcher. However, it would be well to read the "Starting Point" under the Theoretical Method, as this will, perhaps unconsciously, provide some type of a beginning basis. This presupposes uncertainty, unfamiliarity, lack of knowledge, or desire for additional support, and thus investigation is directed toward the "facts" or "truth." Nevertheless, gathering "all" the facts may be like counting the sands of the seas. One must stop somewhere; the beating of the bushes must cease, and the "foe" must be faced with the resources at hand—hopefully, a skillful hand.

Weighing the Facts

This is the weighing or balancing that eventually leads to a conclusion. Initially, it suggests consideration of a problem from all angles—a complete survey of all available material. The degree of objectivity possible will be in direct proportion to the thoroughness of research.

Proposing Solutions

This may include on the one hand what is possible (the more inclusive term) which does, or may, exist or occur, as against, on the other hand, that which is practicable (more selective solution).

Selection of a Solution, Conclusion, or Both

Here one needs to be discriminate and objective. One must distinguish and select the "best." It implies penetration of the surface, judging what is the best and presenting it forcefully.

Suggesting a Means for Achieving Part IV

The primary concern here is to present a clear and convincing means to others. It involves salesmanship.

Suggested sample subjects and titles:

Creative Literature for Study of the Family
How to Fight High School Drop Outs in Rural Areas

How to Motivate College Freshmen
Revolutionary Methods of Teaching Children Reading
The Value of the Two Year College

The Experimental Method

Religious faith begins as an experiment, moves forward through experience and becomes verified progressively as we continue to attest to its validity. This faith stands or falls on the noblest hypotheses. Experiment implies some degree of control while moving from the simple to the complex. As the comment above on faith suggests, experimentation is a valid method for disciplines other than pure science. The essentials of almost any sort of experimental study can be expressed in three headings:

I. Hypothesis or Theory
II. Experience
III. Conclusion

The Hypothesis or Theory

Tentative acceptance is implied in an assumed premise; it serves as a point of departure for discussion. The hypothesis may also be a conclusion to a research paper, being offered as the most reasonable explanation of certain phenomena. One may also begin with a theory. This presupposes more supporting evidence and a greater likelihood of truth than the former and suggests that it deserves acceptance. Likewise, a theory may be a conclusion to a research paper.

Experience

Either observation is involved or actual participation occasionally is gained through another's experience. Experience finds out facts, procedures, and apparatus used. It gathers and assembles such data. In the experience area, control functions, and the degree of control applied to the given situation takes place. Control, as used here, becomes the means or method that provides a standard of comparison or means of verification.

Conclusion

The consequence of one's initial hypothesis or theory comes into proper perspective. Here you formulate the final or summarizing proposition based on step II, Experience. It may be a result—that which is produced immediately or directly, a direct correlative of "cause." Consequence may be ones conclusion—a logical or natural outcome of steps I and II, but with a looser connection with a cause than with an effect. Regardless of the emphasis of the conclusion, one ought to relate the information obtained to the general field or theory.

Suggested sample subjects and titles:

The Effectiveness of Independent Study at X College
Experiment With Two or More Methods of Teaching Reading
TV Teaching is More Useful than Classroom Methods
Small Group Teaching is Superior to Individual Instruction

The Theoretical Method

The Theoretical usually confines the treatment of a particular subject in such a manner as to exclude the practical, or an application of the knowledge gained. In other words, this method terminates in theory or speculation rather than a practical basis or application. It is concerned with such questions as the following: What is time? What is the direction of human evolution? Is there life on Mars? What is good? What is life? What is humanity? It may compare two or more theories and choose among them. It may be the discussion of a theological doctrine or philosophical viewpoint. An outline of this method would normally suggest:

I. Starting point
II. Ascertaining the Arguments (Pro and Con)
III. Weighing the Arguments (Pro and Con)
IV. Proposing Views
V. Selecting a View

Starting Point

To begin implies a given theory, fact, or support. You begin by taking something for granted, as true, or as existing. This starting point is then used as the basis for reasoning. It may be in the form of an assumption, presupposition, presumption, postulation, position, or premise.

Ascertaining the Arguments (Pro and Con)

Although this may presuppose your unfamiliarity, lack of knowledge, and desire for additional support, it does not necessarily follow that you seek this information objectively. However, objectivity is the aim. Argument, as used here, stresses the appeal to evidence and the reasoning used to support your claims. It is a means used to prove your case and convince your opponents. It will conclude both philosophical and theoretical views.

Weighing the Arguments (Pro and Con)

The starting point may again affect your "weighing" of the arguments. Selective gathering of facts to support a prejudgment would preclude any objective weighing of the "facts." Gathering of facts should suggest consideration of a view from all angles, including all supports, facts, and arguments.

Proposing Views

Here you put forth or attest to the validity, genuineness, fallacy, or inoperability of various views.

Selecting a view

This projects a particular view as being the most logical or reasonable, along with the underlying supports for such view. The emphasis here is on persuasion—to present clearly and convincingly your view to others.

The theoretical could also suggest an organizational approach similar to that of the unfolding method.

You must be careful here not to force the above basic organizational methods of approaching research so rigidly that you are restricted as you proceed. These are only suggestive of overall concepts which must be faced before procedure is possible with any systematic research project.

Suggested sample subjects and titles:

Is There a Theory of Literature?
Theories of Poetics
Theories of Religious Belief
Is There a God?
Social Science Methodology
Are Flying Saucers Tenable?

RECORDING THE FINDINGS

There is no logical step by which all individuals ought to proceed, for each person's thought patterns may differ. For clarity, therefore, the next two chapters are separated. One may prefer to read the next two chapters on outlining and note-taking in reverse order as note-taking and the early stages of outlining are intermingled and cannot be totally separated.

A proper note system for both bibliography and content notes is a prerequisite to efficient organization of a research paper. The following suggestions will prove most useful and should be thoroughly understood before you begin search for materials. Failure to do this will cost needless hours of time and produce a paper of less than your potential.

Briefly, the bibliography notes will be used to indicate at the end of your research paper a list of all materials used to compile information on your particular subject—usually consisting of the author, title, date, and publisher. The content notes provide the substance with which you build your research paper. It may consist of a summary, a paraphrase, a direct quotation, or a combination of these.

Recording what you read, or note-taking, is a skilled activity requiring arduous practice. However, the results are of great value. Note cards serve the researcher in a number of ways:

1. To recall what one reads.
2. To make main points available for later use in a convenient form.
3. To help you organize material for a paper, for notes can be shuffled like playing cards.
4. To provide material which may not be readily available later.
5. To provide information needed for citing sources in your paper.
6. To provide bibliographic information.

Now we turn to the mechanics, the characteristics of good note-taking, and the mental processes involved in note-taking.

Plagiarism

Before proceeding, a further comment about note-taking must be emphasized when using another's material for a research paper. Failure to give proper credit in one's paper for the essential material of another person is plagiarism—implicitly implying that you are crediting to yourself the language, ideas, and thoughts of another are your original work. Many students have failed courses or have been asked to leave college for plagiarism. However, the fine line cannot always be drawn between deliberate or accidental copying and innocent improvement upon another's words. Unconscious plagiarism may occur after you read material, especially that with which you agree. Even after digesting, integrating, and reorganizing ideas, when ideas come out in writing you may reproduce much the same idea and wording as someone that you recently read. Some things fall in the area of "common" knowledge or "public domain," and therefore, need not be cited. Occasionally, research scientists, through independent study and experimentation, arrive at the same conclusion. There are times when the distinction between borrowed thinking and that of your own is definitely unclear. Montaigne has aptly put it: "Though old the thought and oft exprest, Tis his at last who says it best." Another has put it: "The bees plunder the flowers here and there; but afterward they produce the honey, which is peculiarly their own."

Format of Note Cards

Bibliography Note Cards

The bibliography note card (a card used to record sources consulted) is patterned after the basic order (see under "Bibliography" in Supplementary Pages). Following the order of this card makes possible for easy alphabetization of data in the exact order needed for the bibliography. The eight points insure against omission of essentials. Many researchers have lost much valuable time retracing steps to locate a source because they overlooked information when first recording the source. The importance of this card cannot be overemphasized if you wish to save time. Carry with you a sample (reminder) guide card for the bibliography note card. It should contain the following information:

Sample Guide Card for Bibliography

1. Author (last name first).
2. Date.
3. Title,
4. Initiator,
5. (Special note)
6. Components,
7. Publisher and place.
8. Total pages or inclusive pages

Miscellaneous Information—

This card will serve as a reminder of the essentials to record about all sources used.

Complete each bibliography note card in a similar manner to that below. The following is an example of a completed bibliography note card:

1. Winchell, Constance M.	REF
2. 1967	Z
3. Guide to Reference Books	1035
4.	W 79
5.	1967
6. 8th ed.	M.S.U.
7. American Library Association, Chicago, Ill.	
8. 741 pages	

The information taken from the preceding sample card can be transferred directly to your bibliography after all bibliography note cards have been alphabetized by author in the exact order required:

Winchell, Constance M.
1967. Guide to Reference Books, 8th ed., Amer. Lib. Assoc., Chicago, Ill., 741 pp.

The following points should also be remembered if you wish efficiency in bibliography note taking.

Use 3x5 or 5x8 cards. Different colors may be useful to indicate particular categories of material. Use only one size card.

Make out a card if you think the material will contribute to your investigation.

Note on the card all bibliographical information possible. It is better to take more information than is needed.

Include on the card the name of the particular library (if using more than one) where the material was found, and the book's call number in the event later rechecking is necessary.

On the back of the card you may wish to summarize the author's qualifications, his general point of view, and your evaluation of the contribution this material makes to your investigation. This information can serve in making an annotated bibliography later in case one is required. An annotation consists of a brief nature and content of the work, its relationships to present study, and general use to others. It is usually less than 50 words.

Keep these cards filed alphabetically by author in the order they will appear in the bibliography.

Several articles or books by the same author (published in the same year), differentiate among them by adding an "a," "b," etc. to the publishing date, i.e., 1954a.

Content Note Card

Use a handy size card (3x5 to 5x8) or pad of paper. Whatever size you use, be consistent. Different colored cards may prove useful to indicate types of materials, etc. Five points should always be observed when making a content note:

Cite the exact source—In the upper left hand corner of the note card, give the author's last name, date and page(s) i.e., (Smith, 1946, 34) or in the case no author is given, the title i.e., (Crimes of Violence, 1967, 123). The remainder of one's material will be on the Bibliography note card.

Limit one point to one card—The other side of the card may be used to complete a note. Remember that the cost of cards is less than the cost of time and confusion later when organizing one's paper.

Assign a subject heading describing the general content of the note on each card—Place the heading in the upper right hand corner of the card. As the tentative outline of your paper takes shape, the headings can be increasingly specific. The value of this labeling will become more apparent when all the material has been gathered and preparation is made to write the paper.

Indicate type of material in note card—Use of quotation marks indicates a direct quotation. Be sure to include the page(s) of the quote. Also, indicate on the card whether the material is a paraphrase or your own "idea."

Abbreviations—Use of abbreviations (meaningful to you) greatly reduce the time of note-taking. Skill in this matter may be attained through study and use of good synonyms and usage dictionaries.

(Sample)
Content Note Card

Subject heading

(Smith, 1964, 122-123) Enrollment

"Contents note ------

-----------."

Degree of Achievement and Time Spent In Note-taking

Before taking any notes, if at all possible, read a summary article of your topic in an encyclopedia or general reference work in that specific field. The purpose here is to help you recognize important points as they turn up in further reading i.e., dates, bibliographies, names, etc. It may also help you to recognize points of difference or unusual ideas which might be discussed in individual sources. Often, a tentative outline at this point will help. This outline may well be just that of the summary article you have read. If you are familiar with your subject, you can proceed by making a tentative outline before you begin taking notes. However, this should be done with caution for it may tend to prejudice your conclusion by causing you to fit your materials to your outline.

Your particular approach to sources will determine the degree of achievement and time spent. Factors affecting both time and achievement in reading and note taking are:

1. The level of detail desired.
2. The degree of thought with which you respond to the material. Does it produce original thinking, questions, answers, etc, or do you merely produce the author's point of view? Reading and thinking are the keys to good notes. Only strict concentration will enable you to formulate questions and recognize the answers as they come.
3. The brevity of notes used to record what is read (this assumes clarity of these notes at a later date)

What is Desired?

The level of detail desired involves two aspects. First, you must know clearly just what is needed: statistics, general information, the amount of information, current data, biographical materials, etc. A few minutes thought here will save hours of searching. Second, you must determine the usefulness of a given source before consuming an undue amount of time on it.

After locating material which seems to relate to your subject, first try to get an overview of its theme and scope. In the case of a complete book, read all prefatory material, table of contents; scan the text, reading the opening and concluding paragraphs of each chapter. This will help you to evaluate immediately the value of the material.

The value of short articles or chapters of a book may be determined much the same way as a whole book, but more intensively. Note any headings in the text because they are placed there for emphasis. Note particularly the first and last sentence in each paragraph, and if necessary, jot down a brief summary note on each until you become skilled at this. This type of skimming is essential as it will both help prevent the reader from mere paraphrasing and also helping him to evaluate as he reads the material more thoroughly. This skimming is a prelude to studying, not a substitute for it.

Whether the material is a lengthy book or a relatively short article, this scanning of the text will help one to become aware of the author's organizational plan. This is essential to a good understanding of the author's work. It is well worth noting that one will need to do more reading and note-taking than will appear in the final paper. It is impossible to tell at this point exactly the final limitations of the paper.

Responding to the Material

What should you look for when reading? What "cues" help determine the author's emphasis? What signals should you watch for? The following points should be looked for specifically until they become an unconscious part of your reading:

Boldface type heading in a chapter indicates important ideas essential to explanation of the salient point.

Key sentences:

1. Introductory sentence—announcement-making.
2. Transition sentence—author indicates he is about to present another important idea—he is leading into the next point.
3. Concluding sentence –a kind of summarizing.

Major points will be followed by a series of supporting points.

Repetition of a point indicates the author's emphasis.

The significance of certain words and what they may indicate are important in reflecting the correct ideas of the author.

Length of Note

The next important step is to evaluate and digest what you have read for the preparation of a note. This involves selecting and grouping essentials, ideas, and related details.

State main idea or central thesis. Write down just enough supporting fact, detail, or example to clarify the central theme. Isolate principal subordinate ideas. Note interpretations, implications, applications, and the significance of what you read. Discriminate between fact and opinion, established principles and speculative guessing. Be alert to instances in which different authorities agree or disagree. Back your opinions with data. Give greater weight to authors who cite evidence for their conclusions than to those who merely make dogmatic assertions. Indicate on cards best sources, those contradicting one another, and other information helpful to show a particular work's authority.

Types of Content Notes

On evaluation, each note will tend to fall into one of four types: the summary note, paraphrase note, direct quotation note, or a combination of these.

Precis (Summary or Abstract Notes)

These present only the bare outline, the main points, probably without details. *Usually* no specific source is cited in this type of note. However, if you refer to any general or specific statement or point of view of someone else, you should show support by referring to the source, i.e., briefly, Smith's views are. . . .[2] This reference may not be to a specific page but only to a book or article as a whole.

The summary note may be in a running outline form or abstract—summarizing only its essential points. It is a condensation, a summarizing of essential points, or a selected title or topic sentence which summarizes an entire article. It is an attempt to draw out the essential from the unessential by omitting most of the merely illustrative content of the original article. There are both rules and dangers in abstracting and summarizing.

Rules to observe:

1. Present ideas of the original accurately.
2. Be brief.
3. Be clear in presenting the essence of the original meaning.
4. Present the essential parts completely.

Dangers to expect:

1. For every increase in efficiency (brevity) we pay with a corresponding decrease in meaning. One must maintain a balance between efficiency and meaning.
2. Because of one's need for more meaning than his notes contain (due to brevity and generalizations), it may cause him to credit the notes with meaning they do not have.

Bear in mind the points just covered under "Responding to the Material" if you expect to make good summary notes. Otherwise notes will become mere paraphrases of the original author's words, crediting them to oneself. This is little more than plagiarism, even when this is not the intent of the note-taker. Getting an overview of the material, looking for "cues" which help determine the author's point of view, evaluating and digesting what you have read are essential to summarizing what you read.

Paraphrase Notes

A paraphrase renders another person's ideas but not his exact words. It is a simplifying and/or amplifying, as well as interpretative rendering of the sense of a difficult passage. It usually covers only a brief passage. A careful paraphrase is usually preferable to a lengthy quotation. Although paraphrases are not enclosed in quotation marks, acknowledgment must be given to the source, including pages. There are four types of materials which may call for paraphrasing.

1. Scholarly articles needing simplification
2. A very condensed style of writing needing amplification
3. Unfamiliar language in older writings
4. Obscure or figurative writing needing to be rendered into plain or literal expressions.

Avoid misrepresentation of the author's original meaning by substituting words which change the original meaning. Make a note on your card that this is a paraphrase.

Direct Quotation Note

> A fine quotation is a diamond on the
> finger of a man of wit, and a pebble
> in the hand of a fool—Joseph Roux

This is reproducing exactly the words of another (including punctuation and spelling), giving credit to the author and/or source. The exact source must be cited. It may be asked, "Why and when should one quote?"

1. When the exact wording is significant
2. When a point needs substantiation by citing an accepted authority—one that carries weight
3. When consciseness is desirable and the passage, if reworded, would be lengthened thereby
4. When you wish to amplify a discussion by presenting the same or differing views held by others
5. When a passage becomes less expressive or graphic by summarizing or paraphrasing
6. When references are to laws, official rulings, or edicts
7. When citing scientific, mathematical, or other formulas

Use quotations sparingly so you vary and present original thinking. Avoid quoting the obvious. However, there are times when a detailed analysis of the works of an author, or for other valid reasons, extensive use of quotations is required.

Brief quotations, such as a line of poetry or short paragraph (less than 8 lines) should be included in quotation marks as a part of the text, unless emphasis is needed.

Lengthy quotations (eight or more lines, two or more lines in the case of poetry) should be separated from the text with slight indentation (5 spaces) on the left margin and single spaced. Lengthy quotations may require asking permission to quote. The copyright period in the U. S. is normally 56 years. Much time can be saved by using a photoduplication service rather than copying lengthy passages by longhand. Be sure to add to the top or back of a photocopy the source of information. An exceptionally long quotation, exceeding one page, may be placed in the appendix and referred to at the proper place in one's paper (see example below illustrating sample text followed by an appendix sample).

(From the text of a paper)

. . . to those who hold the view which argues that in principle a democracy is justifiied in denying political privileges to those who would destroy it, the words of Sidney Hook[1] are well addressed. Their arguments add up to retaining democracy, not an argument against permitting agitation for the destruction of democracy. . . .

[1] (See Appendix I)

Appendix I

"Those who believe in tolerance must, if they are sincere, be opposed to intolerance. To be opposed to intolerance certainly requires that any *acts* of intolerance be prevented or punished; it may even require that incitement to intolerance . . ." (Hook, 1962, 134-139)

Miscellaneous—Parallels of two or more texts should be arranged in columns, with alignment indicated. Interviews, lectures, speeches, should be submitted for approval of the person making the statement before incorporating in your paper.

Amount of Notes, Note Editing, and Follow-up

Write just enough to get the point pinned down and make possible recalling the ideas later. As you gather material and look for an overall picture of your topic, a tentative outline will begin to form. As the outline takes form, it will become apparent whether or not enough material has been collected for each part of the topic.

Taking good notes and comprehending the material read, however, does not insure retention of the material. An important part of note-taking is re-reading them soon—within a few hours after taking them to assure yourself of the meaning. This calls for editing so they will mean something to you a week later. The sooner you edit your notes, the easier your task of composing your paper. Finally, reflection on your notes is necessary before writing a paper. Reflection is a necessary step in making the ideas and facts your own. Spontaneously and subconsciously thinking goes on during this whole process of collecting information. There must be time to take advantage of this type of reflection. This means you must start research far in advance of due date. The procrastinating student is ever struggling with failure.

A final word to note-taking. Let it not be said of you:
"There's not a note of mine that's worth the noting." Shakespeare

OUTLINING

One of the most valuable gains from a research paper for the undergraduate is the ability to organize material. The table of contents of a book is usually an outline of the book, and presents the scheme by which the author divided his subject. In short, the outline is a plan showing the relative importance and relationships of ideas. It is analogous to a map or a blueprint.

Up to this point, the notes taken for a paper are most likely in an unorganized, run on outline—an accumulation of unrelated ideas and facts. But before we discuss the outline itself further, we should suggest reasons why one should make so much ado about outlining.

Justification for Outlining

Beginning Stages

1. It helps get your plan out of your mind and onto paper.
2. It gives an idea of the main points to be developed—a preliminary plan.
3. It helps select a controlling idea or thesis.
4. It is needed to achieve continuity.
5. It helps divide a subject so that you can concentrate on one part at a time.
6. It helps label notes.

Developing Stage

1. It helps determine what specifics to look for during additional reading; it may indicate gaps.
2. It helps distinguish and select points which are relevant.
3. It helps identify ideas and their relationships.
4. It prevents wandering from the subject.
5. It keeps one from including material not applicable.
6. It prevents from placing material in the improper place.

Concluding Stage

1. It saves hours of rewriting and eliminates errors in organization.
2. It guides the writer in a clear, logical and comprensive manner.

3. It provides a final formal outline, enabling both writer and reader to see at a glance the over-all plan and logic of the entire paper.

A Controlling Statement

Basic to a tentative outline is the controlling idea, thesis, or hypothesis. It is more than the subject itself—it is an idea based on a subject. The idea or thesis is reached when the subject is restricted enough to be reasonable and challenging. Essentially, you have a thesis when you have something to say or prove. Consequently, the greater your conviction and involvement in your statement, the more interest and satisfaction in your research paper. This idea or statement is usually more specific than the phrasing of the topic or subject of the research paper. The point of view must be clear, for the reader will need this to interpret what you say. The controlling idea sets the stage and radically influences both selection of materials and how to organize them. However, preliminary research may even cause one to reject his original statement and select another. This statement of purpose can later be used for appraising all material found on the chosen subject. The controlling statement may or may not be formally stated in an outline or table of contents.

Elements of an Outline

There are generally accepted principles which should be observed in all outlines. However, an outline may be changed several times before the formal or final outline is completed.

Two means are used in conventional outlines to show relationships: alternating of numbers and letters, and indention. These indicate the rank of the headings, those with the least indention and those with the greater symbol, being the most important. The order of importance from greater to lesser are Roman numerals, capital letters, Arabic numerals, and small letters:

I. HEADING
    A. Subheading
        1. Sub-point
        2. Sub-point
            a. Sub-section
            b. Sub-section
    B. Sub-heading
        1. Sub-point
        2. Sub-point

II. HEADING
   A. Sub-heading
   B. Sub-heading
   C. Sub-heading
      1. Sub-point
      2. Sub-point

Note that the final copy of the outline, when used as the Table of Contents, uses only the Roman numerals to indicate chapter headings.

Indent subheadings under a chapter, two spaces from the beginning of a chapter title. (See sample Tables of Contents.)

Headings, when designated by the same kind number (I, II, III), must be of approximately equal importance. This would also apply to subheadings, such as (A, B, C) or (1, 2, 3). Be careful not to place subordinate materials in the same rank as important material nor vice versa.

Headings of equal rank or importance (I, II, III), should have a connecting element (implied or expressed) which relates them to each other. Likewise, the subheadings, A, B, C, should relate to the main headings I, II, III, in casual relationship.

Subheadings under a given heading should be expressed in identical structural form—all phrases, words, or sentences. However, rigid conformity must not be adhered to in all cases, or more time must be spent on the outline than the paper itself.

Have at least two subdivisions for any heading which has subdivisions. Usually a subdivision, if only one, may be expressed in the main topic heading if it is important, or it may be accompanied by another subtopic. There are but two exceptions to this rule. An example which is used to develop a particular heading may be listed by itself:

II. THE LANGUAGE OF THE ESSAY (main heading)
   A. "The Business of an Essayist" by William P. Fields (sub-heading)

Also, a prepositional outline may have only one subdivision. This is illustrated under "The Sentence Outline." Do not burden an outline with superfluous details, illustrations, examples, etc. If a topic takes up more than one line, the continuation should start even with the first line. Avoid undue subordination in an outline if it would take less than a paragraph to develop. Strive for consistency in the extent to which a main heading is subdivided; maintain a balance. Categories of an outline should not overlap.

Steps in Outlining

Tentative Outline

At the beginning, it may be merely first impressions or almost an unconscious linking together of ideas as you read. However, many people accumulate a number of ideas which need to be organized. To get started, you must jot down all the ideas you have about your topic. Look them over to evaluate their relations. A little planning here will help avoid "hodgepodge." The chapter on "The Approach" was intended to help in this initial stage. This beginning will logically lead to a tentative outline of possible headings. A tentative outline is only a means to an end; it is never an end in itself.

The purpose of the tentative outline is to keep you mindful of the focus and organizational plan as it develops. It also enables you to label notes with subject headings from an outline, which will help fit them into the over-all plan of the research paper. Nevertheless, this tentative outline can be dangerous; use it with caution and avoid anything that might tend to prejudice conclusions —causing you to "fit" materials to your outline. Be the master of the outline, not a slave to it.

Working Outline

The working outline is simply an amplification of the tentative outline. It should use the basic symbols and other devices of a formal outline (See: Elements of an Outline). This becomes a working plan and should be flexible. You must juggle ideas until the easiest continuity is achieved. This means continuous revision, adding or eliminating topics, rearranging the order, and re-evaluating headings. This outline adjusting will not reach its final form until the reading and note-taking are finished.

Final or Formal Outline

This final outline is intended primarily for the reader but enables both reader and writer to see at a glance the plan and logic of the whole research paper. It shows the order, the unity, and the relative importance of various parts of a research paper.

The following points must be observed:

1. It should follow the accepted conventions of outlining as listed earlier under "Elements of an Outline."
2. It should be completed only after the final draft of the research paper.
3. It reduces the body of material to its essentials, and is less detailed than a tentative or working outline.

4. This final outline also becomes a final check on the continuity of a completed paper. It may reveal the undesirable, which may go undetected in the writing, but be flagrantly obvious in outlining.

Types of Outlines

All outlining falls into three basic types: topic, sentence, and paragraph. It is important, however, to point out that the type of outline one prefers is not as important as its continuity or inherent logic. The same general theme or topic has been used for each type in the following examples in order to more clearly illustrate differences and parallels.

The Paragraph Outline

It is normally used as a preliminary outline, and later reduced to a topic or sentence outline.

GROUNDS FOR CHRISTIAN HUMILITY

INTRODUCTION: The meaning of humility is often misunderstood, especially Christian humility. There is a sharp difference between the Biblical and the non-Biblical use of this term.

I. The roots of humility are found in the Person and teachings of Jesus Christ. His early disciples, though imperfectly, exemplified His humility.

II. Although humility is superficially linked with lack of manliness, Christian humility demands courage. Manliness is considered desirable by everyone. As Christians view humility, it is consistent with manliness and is, in fact, an element of manliness.

III. Humility is dependent, and for the Christian this dependence must be on Christ. A continuing dependence on Christ is essential to producing true humility in the believer.

CONCLUSION: Christ is the Source of this "proper" humility. He is also, to Christians, the Sustainer of true humility.

The Sentence Outline

All headings and further divisions are expressed in complete sentences. The advantages are that it gives more detail and information. Some writers suggest a sentence-topic outline—a combination with major topics as complete sentences, and subtopics as words or phrases. However, most agree that headings and subheadings should be expressed in identical form.

GROUNDS FOR CHRISTIAN HUMILITY

INTRODUCTION: The distinction between Biblical and non-Biblical definitions is great.

I. THE ROOTS OF TRUE HUMILITY ARE FOUND IN A PERSON.
  A. Christ is the Supreme Example of humility.
  B. Christ's disciples demonstrated humility.

II. THE CHARACTER OF CHRISTIAN HUMILITY DEMANDS COURAGE.
  A. Humility is an element of manliness.
  B. Humility is consistent with manliness.

III. CHRISTIAN HUMILITY IS DEPENDENT ON CHRIST.
  A. A continuing dependence on Christ is essential.
  B. Dependence produces true humility.

CONCLUSION: Christ is the Author and Sustainer of Christian humility.

Another form of sentence outline is a "propositional" outline. It is composed of sentences and phrases which either affirm or deny a topic. The examples below illustrate a syllogism in which one premise is unexpressed. This is therefore an exception, spoken of previously, to the generally accepted rule that any heading which has subdivisions must have at least two subdivisions.

GROUNDS FOR CHRISTIAN HUMILITY

INTRODUCTION: Humility defined.

I. CHRIST IS THE SUPREME EXAMPLE OF HUMILITY.
  A. Therefore Christians should be humble.

II. HUMILITY IS NOT ONLY CONSISTENT WITH MANLINESS, BUT IS AN ELEMENT OF MANLINESS.
  A. Therefore Christians should be humble.

III. CHRIST IS THE SOURCE OF ALL POWER.
  A. Therefore Christians should be humble.

The unexpressed premises are: in "I" that Christians are followers of Christ, in "II" that Christians are manly, and in "III" that Christians are dependent on Christ.

The Topical Outline

Headings are brief phrases or single words.

GROUNDS FOR CHRISTIAN HUMILITY

INTRODUCTION: Humility Defined

I. THE ROOTS OF HUMILITY
   A. Christ the example
   B. His followers and humility

II. THE CHARACTER OF HUMILITY
   A. The element of manliness
   B. Consistent with manliness

III. THE CONTINUING NATURE OF HUMILITY
   A. Dependence on Christ
   B. Effect on Christians

CONCLUSION: Christ, the Author and Sustainer

Applications of Outlines

The Subject Itself Is Divided

(Example a)

TIDES

I. WHAT ARE TIDES?
   A. Observing From Shore
   B. Basic Phenomena
   C. Effects of the Wind

II. THE ORIGINS OF TIDES
   A. Newton's Equilibrium Theory
   B. Laplace's Theory
   C. Harmonic Analysis and Prediction of Tides
   D. Characteristics of Tides

III. THE TIDE-GENERATING FORCES
   A. Effects of Moon and Sun
   B. Experimental Demonstration

IV. MEASURING TIDES
   A. Tide Gauges
   B. Tides on Open Seas
   C. Tidal Currents

(Example b)

THE PLANET EARTH

I. GENESIS: THE ORIGIN OF THE EARTH

II. THE LITHOSPHERE
   A. Core and Mantle
      1. The Earth's Interior
      2. The Earth's Heat
      3. The Earth's Magnetism
   B. Crust
      1. The Shape of the Earth
      2. The Crust of the Earth

III. THE HYDROPHERE
   A. Glaciers
   B. The Circulation of the Oceans

IV. THE ATMOSPHERE
   A. The Circulation of the Atmosphere
   B. The Ionosphere

Rhetorical Division (e.g., Introduction, Body, Conclusion)
It is similar to that of a speech.

TOWN "X"

INTRODUCTION
   A. Nature of the Investigation.
   B. The Historical Setting.

I. MAKING A LIVING
   A. The Dominance of Making a Living.
   B. Why do People Work so Hard?

II. CREATING A HOME
   A. The Houses in Which People Live.
   B. Marriage.
   C. Family Life.

III. ACQUIRING AN EDUCATION
   A. Who Goes to School?
   B. Those Who Train the Young.
   C. School Life.

IV. USING LEISURE TIME
   A. Traditional Ways of Spending Leisure.
   B. The Organization of Leisure.

CONCLUSION

A Collection of Related Aspects of a Basic Subject

INDONESIA

I. THE HISTORICAL BACKGROUND
  A. Early History
  B. The Coming of the Westerners
  C. The Rise of Nationalism
II. THE CONTEMPORARY SETTING
  A. The Civil Service and the Army
  B. Economic Structure
III. THE POLITICAL PROCESS
  A. The Ideology of Guided Democracy
  B. The Constitution and Governmental Organization
IV. MAJOR PROBLEMS
  B. National Unity
  C. Foreign Relations

Using the Outline

Think of the beginning phase of writing or communicating in a steady progressive manner. The writing should first emphasize making sense, being logical, reasonable, and authoritative. Next, attention must turn to correctness of the mechanics of writing (punctuation, grammar, spelling, etc.). Move from here to capture the reader's interest and emphasize your individual style. Finally, the general appearance or format must be considered. Further expansion of these points will follow, but first note the four important considerations below, prior to beginning the actual writing of the first draft.

Your notes must be separated into general groups corresponding to the main headings of your outline. The notes must then be labeled more exactingly and headings assigned to notes which have none.

Eliminate superfluous materials. All notes which do not immediately fit must be put aside with the hope that they will be used before the paper is finished. These notes which have been temporarily set aside should be reviewed again after the first draft is completed.

Outline changes may need to be made in order to keep a balance. There must be a balance in material selected for each outline heading and subheading. This may mean either dividing material under one heading into two or more main headings or completely omiting points which cannot be sufficiently developed. This final look at the outline before writing may also require seeking additional material in order to correct gaps or complete points insufficiently developed. This reshuffling or adjusting and readjusting is both normal and desirable with most outlines up to the end.

Communicating with the reader cannot be overemphasized. The primary purpose of the outline is to give the reader an immediate grasp of the whole paper. However, the grasp of the paper's content will be progressive. The writer must thoroughly understand this progression as he attempts to communicate with the reader:

1. The writer must first make contact with the reader. This is accomplished by clearly defining the scope and limitations of the paper—the length and coverage of the topic. Taking special note of the type of reader for whom the research paper is intended is also a means of making contact and determining the amount of detail, vocabulary, etc., to be used. You must give direction as to where you are going as well as produce some anticipation.
2. The writer must be understood by the reader. Basic to this is communicating the point of view from which you write, so that the reader may interpret what is said in the light of your particular point of view. Certainly the clearer and more effective the writing, the more certain the reader will be to get the full value of what has been written.
3. The writer must hold the reader's interest with a reasonable amount of variety in presentation. Usually this involves progressively unfolding or building to the climax—your view or conclusion.

Preliminary pages

OVERVIEW

Before focusing on the preliminary pages the overview of the order of arrangement of the various parts will be helpful.

*1. Title page (followed by a blank page in formal papers)
2. Preface and/or acknowledgments
3. Table of contents
4. List of tables
5. List of illustrations
*6. The text (may include an introduction and conclusion)
7. Division headings (if needed)
8. Supplementary pages
   Appendixes
   *Bibliography
   Index

*These may be the only parts needed in a short paper: title page, text, and bibliography. Perhaps a few facsimile pages of the preliminary pages will illustrate the format far better than verbal description.

TITLE PAGE SAMPLES

(This is a suggested sample title page for a short paper. If your university or college has its own style of title page, it should be followed.)

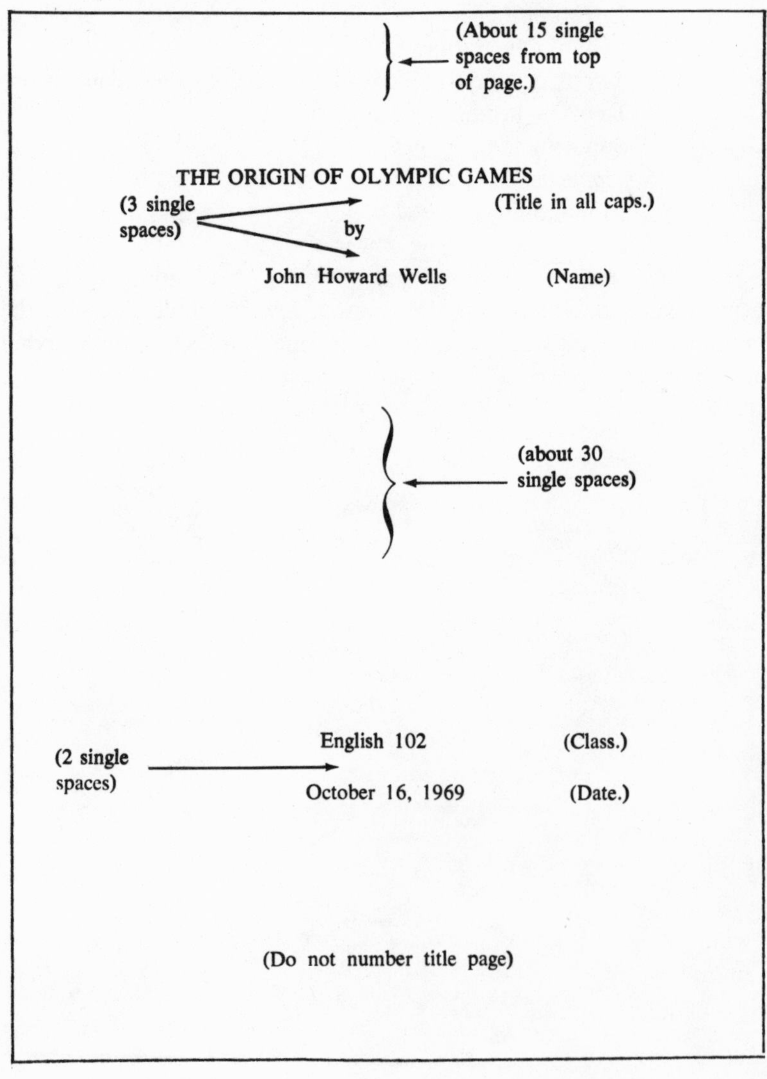

(This is a suggested sample title page for a formal research paper.)

(9-11 single spaces from the top of the page)

TITLE OF RESEARCH PAPER
(If title takes more than one line, double-space and center)

(9-11 single spaces)

A Dissertation (or thesis)
(Double-space) Presented to
the Faculty of the (Dept., School, etc.)
(Name of College or University)

(10-11 single spaces)

In Partial Fulfillment
(Double-space) of the Requirements for the Degree
(Name Degree here)

(7-8 single spaces)

by
(Double-space) Robert John Morris
June 1968

(Do not number title page)

(This is a suggested sample title page for a formal research paper.)

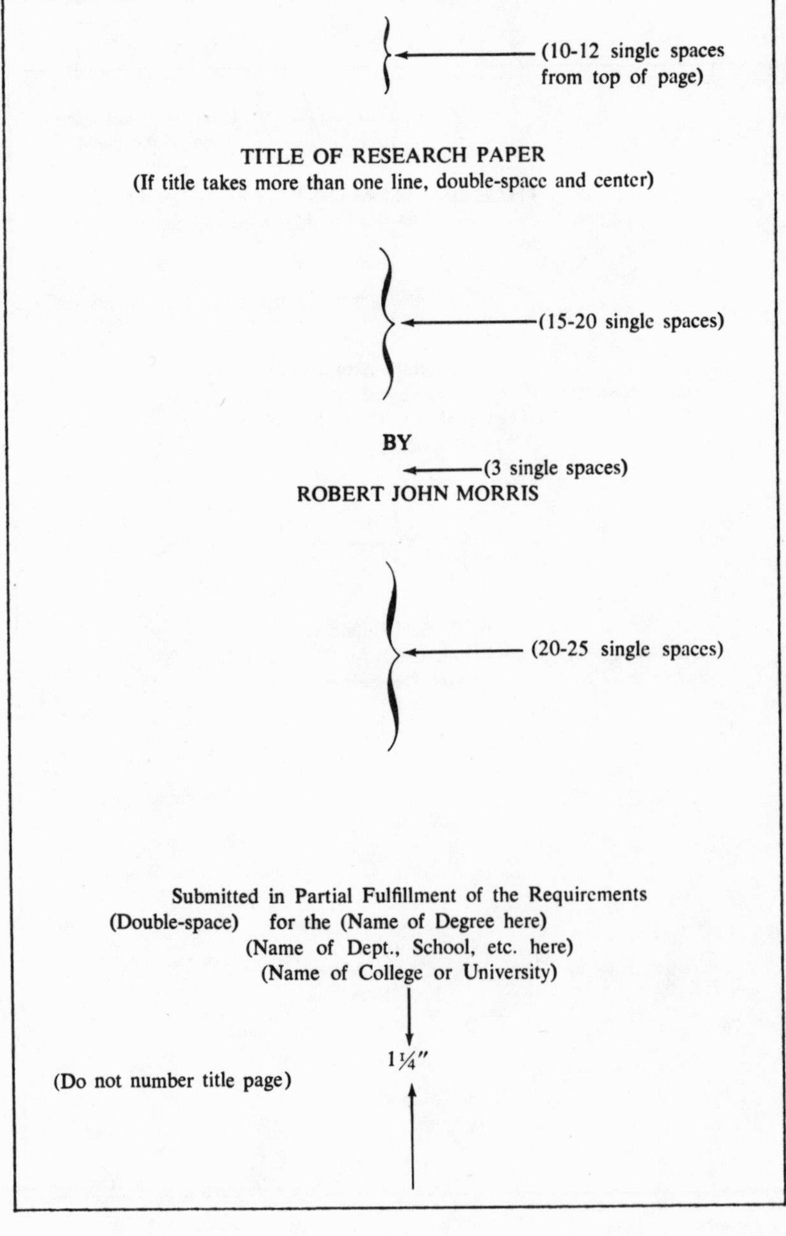

(Follow title page for a formal Research Paper with a blank page (Do not number this page)

PREFACE AND/OR ACKNOWLEDGMENTS SAMPLES

(7 spaces down from top of page)

PREFACE and/or ACKNOWLEDGMENTS

(normally, 4 spaces between heading and text)

(This includes the author's purpose, scope, and acknowledgment of those who aided your research. If both purpose and acknowledgment is given, entitle only "Preface." If you wish only to acknowledge assistance, entitle this page "Acknowledgments." However, this part may be excluded altogether.)

(Number this page in small Roman numerals centered and 1¼″ from bottom of page. Actual page count begins with the title page. Small Roman numerals are used at bottom of all preliminary pages; Arabic numerals begin with the first page of Chapter I and continues throughout the paper, bibliography, appendixes, index, and so forth.)

iii

1¼″

TABLE OF CONTENTS, LIST OF TABLES, AND ILLUSTRATION SAMPLES

The following explains the next few pages of samples.

Center

The table of contents and each part should be centered. If the title is long, set it in two or more double-spaced lines, in inverted pyramid form, all in capitals.

Left Margin

The words "preface," "chapter," "appendix," and "bibliography" begin at the left margin. When alignment is made of Roman numerals, representing chapters, allowance must be made for the largest numeral from the left-hand margin:

PREFACE
CHAPTER
   I.
  II.
 III.
XIII.

Right Margin

Page numbers should be aligned with the right-hand margin.

PAGE
3
10
89
105

Page Numbers

When a half-title page introduces a major subdivision, e.g., Chapter, Bibliography, the Table of Contents lists the page number of the half-title page.

Indention

Indent all subheadings under a chapter, two spaces from the beginning of the chapter title.

The same would apply to any further divisions. When a lengthy heading uses more than one line, the second is indented two spaces from the first line. All subheading letters and Arabic numerals are excluded from an outline when used as a table of contents. The Roman numeral may also be excluded.

Summary and/or Conclusion

If the paper is not divided into parts, as in the previous example, and if you use a formal summary or conclusion, this may be listed as another chapter. In the same table of contents on the following page, the summary or conclusion would be Chapter V.

Table of Contents

The examples given on the following pages are not the only combinations possible but reflect the usual acceptable format. The treatment of the subject, together with the opinion of your professor, may alter these examples somewhat. If additional pages are needed for the contents, omit the contents heading, continuing with the other chapter heading. Never place a major heading at the foot of a page with fewer than two lines of subheadings beneath it.

List of Tables and Illustrations

The examples given reflect the usual, acceptable format.

(7-10 spaces from top)

TABLE OF CONTENTS (or just CONTENTS)

(4 Spaces)

iii

(Use small Roman numeral centered and 1¼″ high from bottom of page)

(7-10 spaces from top)

TABLE OF CONTENTS

(4 Spaces)

(Double-space between sub-divisions)

iii

(Use small Roman numeral centered and 1¼″ high from bottom of page)

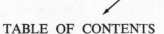

(7-10 spaces from top)

TABLE OF CONTENTS

(4 Spaces)

THESIS: (this is the controlling idea or statement, usually one sentence in length)

(3 Spaces)

iii

(Use small Roman numeral centered and 1¼″ from bottom of page)

(7 spaces from top)

↓

LIST OF TABLES

(4 Spaces)

iv

(Use small Roman numeral centered and 1¼″ from bottom of page)

(7-10 spaces from top)

LIST OF ILLUSTRATIONS

(4 Spaces)

FIGURE PAGE

(3 Spaces)

(When alignment of numbers representing the Figure is made, there must be allowance made for the largest numeral from the left-hand margin. In the above case, "10" and the word "Figure" are in alignment with the margin.)

v

(Use small Roman numeral centered and 1¼″ from bottom of page)

Text

Documentation in a research paper is a must; although the work involved in the mechanics of it are out of proportion to what is gained, this seemingly needless busywork is justifiable. A document may be anything (usually in writing) which offers proof for what one is saying or lends support for a point of view. Documentation is the identification of evidence and support. In a research paper one must use evidence drawn from a wide variety of sources to back conclusions. The variety and number of sources used will be directly related to the nature of the paper's content, the required length of the paper, and the amount of time allowed for its completion.

Briefly, the purpose of documentation is twofold:

1. To demonstrate one's ability to discover useful sources of information (libraries are the primary providers of sources); the bibliography helps indicate the thoroughness of one's search for materials.
2. To indicate accurately the origin of the sources of one's selections, making it possible for the reader to locate the source.

Documentation, as utilized here, is composed of three parts:

1. The Citation Notes—specific references to material included in the text of the paper or referred to therein.
2. The Content Footnote—used for material important enough to include, but whose inclusion would break the trend of thought if contained in the body of the text.
3. The Bibliography—a list of materials used on the topic.

The first two above parts of documentation will be elaborated on and illustrated below. The third point, the bibliography, will be discussed under "Supplementary Pages." These points will supply one with the essentials for documenting all research materials.

Citation Note

The primary purpose of the Citation Note is to give the source and acknowledge indebtedness for borrowed material. This note is placed at the foot of the page within parentheses. We here avoid the extremes of citing sources: that of only a number within the text referring to the bibliography, on the one hand, and that of citing the complete entry at the foot of the page.

Although you should ascertain the prevailing practice and preference in the department in which you are involved, the following concise method is recommended because of its ease and clarity. This method of citing not only is advantageous to the writer but also helps the reader to quickly evaluate the authority of the statement, the recency of the source, the pagination. Since sufficient information is given in the Citation Note, there is no need for the reader continually to refer back to the bibliography, if he is familiar with the field of research covered by the paper. If the reader is not familiar with this field of research, however, a complete entry at the foot of the page is of little value.

Content of Citation Note

The content of the Citation Note refers to materials listed in the bibliography and consists of the author's last name, date of publication, and page(s), if needed, of the reference being cited. It is directed to the specific author who is directly responsible for the material cited. The complete entry of the material cited is listed in the bibliography, alphabetically by author. The purpose of the citation note is:

1. To establish the source from which material is drawn.
2. To acknowledge indebtedness for borrowed material.
3. To refer to additional material.
4. To serve as a cross reference to other sections of your paper.

Basic Points

The three basic points of the citation note are treated in detail below, following the citation note example. The reference number from the text is also shown.

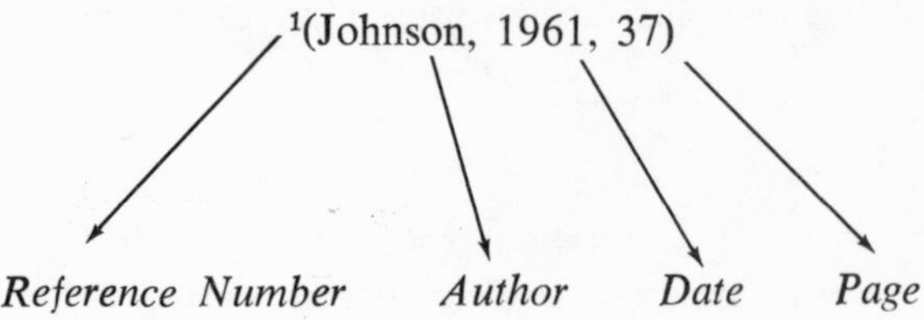

Author—Only the last name is needed unless your bibliography contains more than one person with the same last name; then use initials, i.e., Smith, J.; Smith, M.; Smith, M. B. Unusually long names may be abbreviated.

Publication Date—Only the year is required in the note. When more than one entry are listed in the bibliography under the same author with identical publication dates, they are differentiated by a letter following the date. This differentiation is also given in the citation note:

(Smith, 1966a, 18) (Smith, 1966a, 104)

Page(s)—When a direct quotation or paraphrase is used, pages must be given of the exact source. If several pages are cited from a source which presents a specific view, give inclusive pages: (Smith, 1956, 91-102), or if the reference is to the work as a whole, exclude the pages: (Smith, 1956). Cite the page numbers as 208-211, 96-99, 311-312; not as 208-11, 96-9, 311-12. In case a number (i.e., a legislative bill) is more appropriate than a page, cite as follows: (1966, #2165).

The Location and Form of the Citation Note (see OPTION at end of this section)

The citation note is indicated by a reference number within the body of the text, raised one-half space. The reference number should follow the passage to which it refers, an author's name, a title, a sentence, or a paragraph. The reference number in the text follows all marks of punctuation, if any, except the dash, which it precedes. No space intervenes between the word, or mark of punctuation, and the reference number. The reference number always follows a quotation whether within the text or separated from the text. Reference numbers should follow each other in numerical order on each page, beginning each page with the number one. If the text contains digits where the reference number appears, use a letter or if more appropriate a symbol instead of a number.

Citation notes at the foot of the page are arranged in the same numerical order and must appear on the same page as the reference numbers made in the text. Separate the citation note from the text with a two inch line, beginning at the left margin and one double space below the last line of the text. Indent the first line of each citation note two spaces from the left margin and double space below the two inch line.

The same reference number appearing in the text is repeated at the foot of page, again raised one-half space, with no space before beginning the note:

[1](Smith, 1969, 26)

Two or more citation notes may be placed on the same line, each separated by three spaces. However, never divide a citation note; all entries on any given line must be completed on that line. Begin a new line, double-spaced below the first line indented two spaces for additional citation notes.

[1](Smith, 1969, 26)   [2](Johnson, 1961, 83)   [3](John, 1920)
[4](Evans, 1970, 51)   [5](Brown, 1971, 234)

If the introductory sentence to a quotation includes the author's name, it is not necessary to repeat his name again in the citation note, i.e. (1958, 301).

Various types of needs requiring citation are noted below:

1. Direct Quotation

   Within the text (assuming a short quote) the reference number should follow all marks of punctuation.

   > . . . Referring to the problem of generating terms, he says, "let the documents themselves generate their own uniterms,"[2] In other words, do not start with a pre-

---

[2](Becker, 1966, 78)

2. Separate from the text (assuming a long quote).

Double-space between text & quote. ⟶
Single space quote.

margin 1½″ → from edge of paper

5 sp ⟶ from left margin

On the positive side we have the fact that the number of fragments of fossil hominoid bones that have been described, although relatively small, has increased fairly rapidly in the past thirty years. Against this we have to reckon that the evaluation of most of these remains has been embroiled in much controversy. Here the fundamental difficulty has been that in the great majority of cases the descriptions of the specimens that have been provided by their discoverers have been so turned as to indicate that the fossils in question have some special place or significance in the family or apes. It is so unlikely that they could all enjoy this distinction that, in the circumstances, an outside observer might well imagine that an enterprising anatomist would find little difficulty in substantiating a claim that an artificially fossilized skeletal fragment of any one of the living great apes had a greater relevance to the story of Man's evolution than to that of the skeleton of which it was a part.[1]

---

[1] (Zuckerman, 1958, 301)

Quotation marks are not necessary if the quote is separated from the text, indented five spaces from left margin, and single-spaced.

3. Poetry and drama (two or more lines) are always separated from the text and single-spaced.

a. Drama:

. . . text . . .

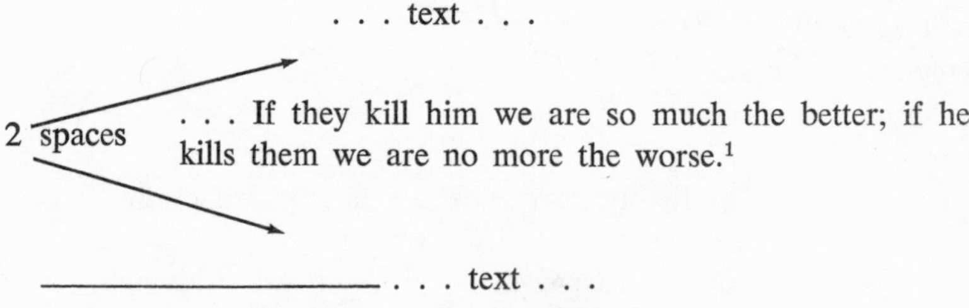

. . . If they kill him we are so much the better; if he kills them we are no more the worse.[1]

. . . text . . .

---

[1] Peter Pan, Act 5, sc. 1 (Barrie, 1928, 81)

Indent five spaces and single space. Quotation marks are not necessary for drama when separated from the text. The title of the play and the specific location within the play are given first. Follow the location by two spaces with the citation note, giving the specific book from which information was taken, along with pagination. If the title of the play has been mentioned previously in the text and is obvious, it need not be repeated at the foot of the page, only the Act, scenes, etc.

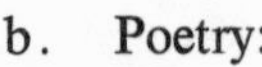

b. Poetry:

. . . text . . .

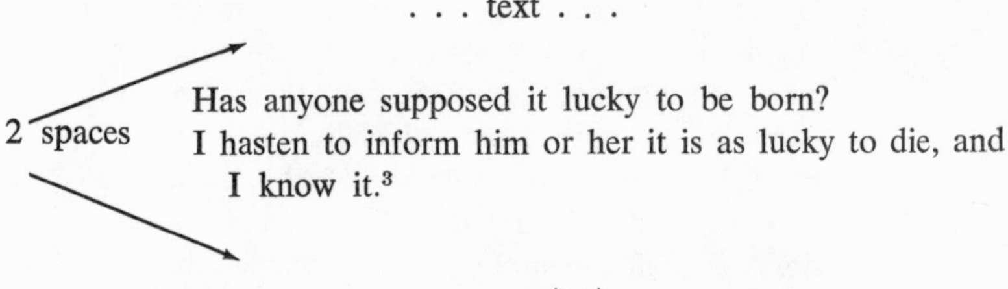

Has anyone supposed it lucky to be born?
I hasten to inform him or her it is as lucky to die, and
  I know it.[3]

. . . text . . .

---

[3] Songs of Myself, Sec. 7, line 122-123 (Whitman, 1955, 75)

Note that if the original line uses more than one line when retyped, the remainder of the line is indented two spaces as noted above with, i.e., "I know it."

Indent five spaces if the lines are lengthy or center the quoted section on the page. Single space and separate from the text two spaces above and below the quote. No quotation marks are needed when separated from the text. At the foot of the page give the title, underlined, and the specific location within the play. Follow this, two spaces, with the citation note giving the specific source this information was taken from, along with pages. There is no need to repeat the title of the poem at the foot of the page if the title has been mentioned in the text previously.

Paraphrase

The reference number is given at the end of the paraphrase. . . . In his conclusion he points out that reliable standards of measurement have not yet been established and pertinent data not yet collected with sufficient care to permit one to reconstruct accurately either cost or performance information in any given instance.[6]

General Reference

This is used when a specific page is not needed, the source being referred to as a whole:

(Erickson, 1944) (Smith, 1926) (Morris, 1967)

If a particular chapter in a book or periodical article is being referred to as a whole, give the inclusive pages:

(Jones, 1938, 45-63) (Smith, J. D., 1964, 18-35)

If the general reference is being made to more than one source, cite as follows:

(Haight, A., 1968; Smith, A., 1967)
(Berry, 1945; Crowell, 1949; Gale, 1956)

The sources are separated by a semicolon (;), and arranged alphabetically by author.

Cross Reference

When referring to another part of your paper, the following form is used (See p. 13) (See Chap. I) (See also p. 23). Underline "See" and "See also." This type of note will only refer to the research paper being written.

Referral

The referral note indicates additional material not used in the paper. The material is referred to in the same manner as "General Reference" above. However, this material must be listed in the bibliography.

Special Problems

1. No Author

Give date, and page only as this will be sufficient information to locate material in the bibliography.

(1934, 23)

The title is never cited unless it would give added authority to your text. In such cases, list the title within the text if possible and appropriate. In some loose-leaf services, a paragraph number is more meaningful than a page number:

> . . . the latest reference to this bill was in the Congressional Index[1] . . .
>
> [1](1971, #1286)

2. No Author or Date

Material lacking both author and date is rare, but occasionally occurs with pamphlets. Include title within text if appropriate or give fully in citation note.

(Impure Drugs Plaque Doctors, 7)

3. Author, but no Date

(Brown, 86)

4. Author's Name too Lengthy

Abbreviate or include within the text.

5. No Page Numbering

Count pages and record as supplied in the following manner (Brackets meaning that the page number is supplied)

(1968 [23])   (Brown, 1934 [8])

Frequent Reference to the Same Source on the Same Page

When on the same page, consecutive references to the same source may be abbreviated in the following manner:

First reference to the source:	[1](Stewart, 1967, 384)
Further references to the source on the same page need only give the page number, or author for a general reference:	[2](415) or [3](425) When referring to a specific page.

Give complete citation note when again referring to the same book the first time on following pages.

The following is a sample of a paper on inflation showing citation notes and gives a brief bibliography for the pages.

INFLATION

. . . The basic problem is how to prevent consumption expenditures from rising in a time of rising incomes. If the trend toward consumption is not lowered, a sharp rise in the prices of consumer goods is unavoidable.

> Bearing in mind the primary problem of war finance is to restrict consumption expenditure when income is rising, the alternate policies for attaining the objective are relatively few in number. . . .[1]

The second method of controlling is through government spending.

> It follows that an increase in government spending will cause inflation only if (1) there does not initially exist sufficient unusual capacity to accomodate the extra demand. . . .[2]

Our country in nearly two centuries, has never seen such an era of chronic inflation as it has in the last two decades. However, there are a number of economists who have given inflation, of one sort or another, the role of aid to economic growth. . . .

Mr. Slichter says, "the tendency for wages to outrun output per manhour is bound to occur in an economy of private enterprise and powerful trade unions."[3] Some feel that the rapid upswing of wages could be controlled through weakening the power of employees by inducing a higher rate of unemployment. . . .

---

[1] (Dillard, 1948, 244) [2] (Cohn, 1955, 249)
[3] (1967, 163)

BIBLIOGRAPHY

Colm, Gerhard.
1955. "The Government Budget and the Nation's Economic Budget," Readings in Fiscal Policy, selected by the American Economic Association, Irwin, Homewood, III.

Dillard, Dudely.
1948 The Economics of John Maynard Keynes, Prentice-Hall, Englewood Cliffs, N. J.

Slichter, Summer H.
1967. "The Case for Creeping Inflation," Readings in Economics, by Paul A. Samuelson, 5th ed., McGraw-Hill, N.Y., N.Y.

2 spaces

The first and second citation notes in the above example page are typical for quotations separated from the text. These two notes include the author, the date, and the page. Because the author is mentioned in the text, the third citation note gives the date and page only.

It should be noted in the bibliography entries listed above that each entry is listed alphabetically by author. Both author and date are used when referring from the text of the paper to the bibliography. Each sample bibliography entry above is single-spaced, two spaces between entries, and punctuated according to the model entry form. See also under Bibliography.

Option

The preferences of the department concerned should always be observed with any variance in format. The option here is that of placing the citation note within the text rather than at the foot of the page.

The citation note within the text will usually be in the same location as the reference number mentioned above, beginning two spaces following all quotation marks, but before all other punctuation marks. The reference number is not used in this case. The form of the citation note remains the same.

Quotations within text

. . . Referring to the problem of generating terms, he says, "let the documents themselves generate their own uniterms" (Becker, 1966, 78). In other words, do not. . . .

Quotations separate from the text, note following quote

> . . . apes had a greater relevance to the story of man's evolution than to that of the skeleton of which it was a part (Zuckerman, 1958, 301).

Note before quotation

Mr. Slichter (1967, 163) says, "the tendency for . . ."

Content Footnote

This Footnote is intended for material important enough to include but which would break the trend of thought if contained in the body of the text. It might include personal opinions or explanatory notes. The Content Footnote is indicated by a number within the body of the text, even in the middle of a sentence and should be raised one-half space. The same number[1] is repeated at the foot of the same page, indented two spaces from the left-hand margin, again raised one-half space, with no space before beginning the note. The Footnote should be single-spaced. If the text contains digits where the Footnote reference appears, use a letter or if more appropriate a symbol instead of a number to indicate the footnote. A line (about two inches long) should separate the main body of the text from the Footnote, as shown. Double-space between both text and the line, and the Footnote.

When insufficient space prevents conclusion of a note that must begin on a particular page, the remainder is carried over to the bottom of the next page under the separation line preceding any notes on that page. References to material located in an appendix should appear at the bottom of the page in the following manner: [8](See Appendix A)

[1] This example is given here to illustrate the correct form. If a source is cited in this note, it should immediately follow, separated by two spaces. (Smith, 1967, 20)

ILLUSTRATIVE MATERIAL

Use illustrative materials only to reinforce or clarify a written statement. Certain generalizations which should be observed can be made which are applicable to the use of all illustrative materials. These will be discussed first, followed by a separate treatment of tables and illustrations.

General Considerations

Simplicity should be the aim. Avoid trying to convey too many ideas and relationships. It must be clear enough to be understood without reference to the written text; likewise, the written text must be clear without referral to any illustrative material. Neatness and ease in reading are also essential.

Illustrative material must always follow the first discussion of it in the text and be numbered consecutively. Normally, place each table or illustration on a separate page. However, if it is unusually short and included with the text, but cannot be fitted on the page which first mentions it, place it on the next page following the first paragraph, leaving three spaces above and below it.

The significant facts or interpretation of the material should be pointed out and discussed in the text. When reference is made to this material within the text, both number and page must be given, i.e., (Table 2, p. 10); Table 3, page 34 . . .; Figure 6, page 19 . . . (Figure 5, p. 8). Use the sample most appropriate to your text. This also means that each page should be numbered on the upper right-hand corner. If a reasonable exception occurs, the sheet must still be counted as a page.

Content notes for illustrative materials are placed two spaces directly below the material (following any notes of explanation), and aligned with the right-hand margin of the table or illustration.

. . . table . . .

(Smith, 1968, 132)

Remember that the reader is primarily interested in conclusions rather than details. BE BRIEF, ACCURATE, CONSISTENT IN STYLE, AND AS ALPHABETICAL OR NUMERICAL AS POSSIBLE. When possible, after making one good figure or table, use a photocopying machine to produce the other copies needed.

Special Problems

If the date when the illustrative material was compiled is not included in the heading or found in the source which you are using, cite the date of the source itself.

Oversize materials: If it is not possible to keep at least one and one-half inch margin on the left-hand (or binding) side, and one inch margins on the other three sides, one of the following methods is recommended:

1. Place the material on page broadside, the top of material to the left or on the binding side.
2. Reduce the sheet by folding into the research paper. When folding it, be sure to fold so that when it is completely folded there is a one inch margin on the binding side and a one-half inch margin left on the other three edges between

the oversized table and that of the regular paper (8½"x11"). This is needed to prevent cutting the table if the research paper is to be trimmed in the binding process.

3. Photostatically reduce oversize illustrations to standard 8½"x11" size or smaller to allow for heading. The heading and/or page number may have to be typed on a separate paper and glued to the photograph, since one cannot type well on a photograph. Another method which is less expensive is to reduce illustrations by use of special Xerox machines.

It may be necessary to alter some of the spacing suggested in illustrative materials. It is difficult to anticipate all types of materials which might be used and therefore you must judge your unique situation by two factors: consistency and appearance. Alterations of the following rules must be made only for the sake of clarity.

If photographic reduction is undesirable and there is no room for a heading or caption, center the heading or caption on a preceding half-title page in all capitals.

Tables

Statistical data, unless brief, is usually organized in the form of tables. This includes all itemized listings involving tabulations. A list of specific sources are given at the end of this section where various types of tables will be found.

Only closely related data should be represented in a single table.

Number tables consecutively, using Arabic numerals and the word TABLE, in full capital letters, followed by the appropriate number, i.e., TABLE 3.

Captions or titles are given to each table telling concisely what it contains. They are in FULL CAPS and CENTERED ABOVE the table and single spaced.

TABLE 4, INDEX OF PERIODICAL PRICES BY CATEGORY,
1961-1965

Column captions should be given to each column and should be centered and single spaced in the space allotted to its column. Abbreviations may be used when needed and if clear. Clarity and proportion are the criteria for spacing.

TABLE 11. BOOK IMPORTS

(2 Spaces)

Category	1964 New Books	1964 New Editions	1964 Totals	1965 New Books	1965 New Editions	1965 Totals
Art	88	15	103	84	20	104

When a heading is exceptionally long or room is lacking on the page, it may run diagonally upward and to the right from the column, or vertically. (See list of sources where examples of tables may be found.)

Number all columns if frequent reference to specific columns is made. Enclose numbers in parentheses.

TABLE 1. ENROLLMENT IN VOCATIONAL CLASSES, BY TYPE OF PROGRAM FOR SELECTED YEARS

Year (1)	Total (2)	Agri-culture (3)	Distributive occupations (4)	Home economics (5)	Trades and industry (6)	Practical nursing (7)
1962	4,072,677	832,551	331,005	1,730,671	1,052,196	48,976

Miscellaneous aspects of columns:

1. Words—aligned on the left:

   Farm products
   Processed foods
   Textile products and apparel

2. Numbers—aligned on the right:

   201,321
   1,339
   106
   33,125
   23

   If there are decimals, it must be aligned on the decimal points:

   12.1
   8.25
   53.525

3. Dollar sign—use only before the first and last figures (total):

   $ 22.50
   10.00
   8.20
   $ 40.70

4. Degrees—Use only after the first figure:

   78°
   71
   95

5. Omitted item—leave a blank space. However, if this will cause confusion use dots or dashes:

(without dots)

131	324	912
137	132	
48		319
13	78	425

(with dots)

31	...	43	...	...
...	...	...	22	...
45	...	...	...	5
...	...	...	166	...

6. Lines—double horizontal lines should be placed at the top and bottom of a table. Use vertical lines only if clarity is needed. Normally omit all horizontal lines except a single line below the column headings.

Tables covering more than one page should be continued on the next page(s) as follows:

First page of table—

TABLE 4. REPRESENTATIVE LIBRARY CONSTRUCTION PROJECTS PARTIALLY FUNDED UNDER THE HIGHER EDUCATION FACILITIES ACT OF 1963 AS OF JUNE 30, 1965, AGGREGATE U.S.

Second page and those following either include a brief title or just the table and continued—

TABLE 4. REPRESENTATIVE LIBRARY CONSTRUCTION PROJECTS (Continued)

or

TABLE 4. (Continued)

If the continuation of the table is because of its width, it may be necessary to repeat the headings of the first column (left-hand side) in the right-hand side for easy reading and comparison:

TABLE 5. GROUNDS FOR DIVORCE

State	Adultery	Cruelty	Desertion	Bigamy	Separation	Violence	State
Alabama	...	...	...	...	yes	yes	Alabama
New Jersey	yes	yes	yes	...	...	...	New Jersey

The entire format, including all column and other headings is repeated on each subsequent page.

Cite the source of your information (2 spaces below table) unless this is your own compilation. The source should be aligned with the right-hand margin of the table.

Note is 2 spaces below table

. . . TABLE . . .

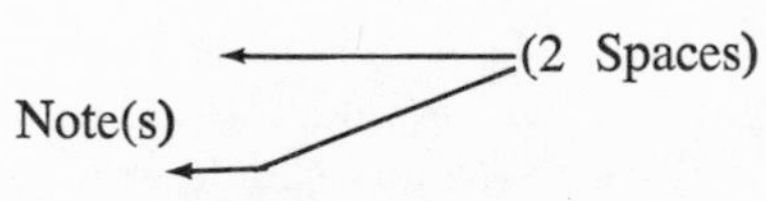

(Source)

The table note is aligned with the left-hand margin of the table. The table note is indicated by a number within the table or heading, raised one-half space. The same number is repeated just below the table, again raised one-half space, followed by one space before beginning the note. The table-note should be single-spaced. If the table contains digits where the reference appears, use a lower case letter instead of a number to indicate the table note. Cite the source of your information two spaces below table note, aligned with the right-hand margin of the table.

List of Table Sources

Most libraries will have all the sources listed below. Note that the examples found in these books should be followed in light of the suggestions given previously in this section. Headings and content notes follow the method given in this text rather than that found in the tables of the suggested sources. Titles only are given as they are the easiest to find in a library card catalog.

Most encyclopedia yearbooks, government documents and dissertations give numerous tables.

Historical Statistics of the United States, Colonial Times to 1957, 1960

Information Please Almanac Atlas and Yearbook (Annual)

Statistical Abstract of the United States (Annual)

The World Almanac and Book of Facts (Annual)

Illustrations

All graphic presentations (charts, photographs, maps, photostats, drawings, etc.) are denoted by the term "Figure." The figures should be numbered consecutively throughout the research paper in Arabic numerals. Each figure must have a caption and only the first letters of principal words should be capitalized. The figure caption should be CENTERED two spaces BELOW the figure as follows:

Figure 7. Effect of Building Configuration on Dispersal of
  Gas Plume.

If the caption is more than one line in length, it should be single-spaced and the carryover should be indented two spaces. All figures should be in black and white—colors should be avoided unless required for the paper by your professor.

Note below figure

. . . ILLUSTRATION . . .

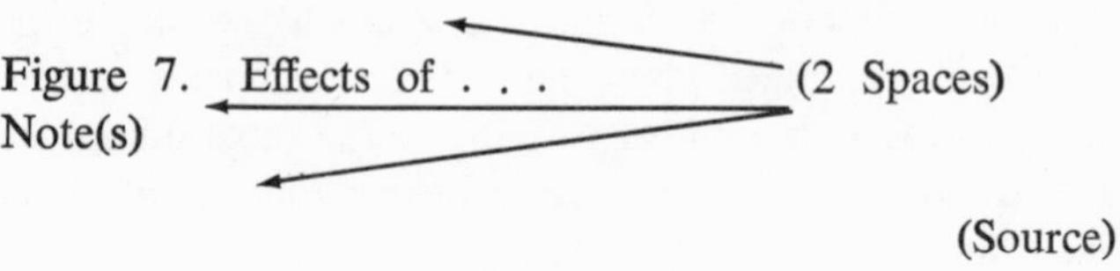

The figure note is aligned with the left-hand margin of the figure. The figure note is indicated by a number within the figure or heading, raised one-half space. The same number is repeated just below the figure heading, again raised one-half space, followed by one space before beginning the note. The figure-note should be single-spaced. If the figure contains digits where the reference appears, use a lower case letter or if more appropriate, a symbol instead of a number to indicate the figure-note. Cite the source of your information two spaces below figure-note, aligned with the right-hand margin of the figure.

Types of illustrations possible for a research paper are almost inexhaustible. The most common forms are discussed below followed by specific sources where examples of these illustrations may be found.

Line or Curve Graphs

They are particularly valuable in showing trends or relationships between two or more (never more than 5) variables. Distinguish between lines representing different data by making them either solid, dotted, dashes, etc., but never by different colors. Reproduction of lines will always be in black and white (printing or photocopying), making different colors useless.

Bar Graphs

The bar graph consists of a series of vertical or horizontal bars arranged to show quantitative relationships. All bars should be of the same width and may be divided into sections. Various points on a given bar should be identified by shading in, hatching, and cross hatching to indicate type of data.

Circular or Pie Chart

It is divided into segments like a pie. Avoid divisions or more than seven parts. Shading of various segments is useful but not always necessary when no more than three segments are represented. When possible, type or print within the segments the information they represent.

Maps

Outline maps are the most satisfactory and should only be used to show geographic location or distribution.

Organization and Flow Charts

These show relationships and/or various parts. The name of each part is included within that designated part (usually a rectangle). Lines and arrows connect each part to show direction or flow or other relationships. The relative level (highest at top) indicates authority and shows subordination. A solid line indicates direct relationships, a broken line indirect relationships.

Mounting of Photographs, etc.

Because of the many possible kinds of illustrations which may need to be mounted, only a few general statements can be made. Use dry mounting tissue (purchasable at any photographic supply store) for mounting purposes. To eliminate wrinkling of paper, type the captions on paper before mounting. Seek technical advice, if necessary, from specialist in duplicating services, architects, art or graphic arts personnel.

NUMBERS WITHIN THE TEXT

	Spell Out	Use Numerals
Dates in general		X
Day of month, but not given	X	
Day of month preceding name of month	X	
Decimals		X
Exact sums of money		X
Fractions	X	X over 3 digits
Frequent use		X
Over three digits		X
"Per cent"	X	
Percentages		X
References to parts of a written work		X
Starting a sentence	X	
Street names	X	
Street numbers		X
Telephone numbers		X
Time of day	X	
		X when A.M. and P.M. used
Under three digits	X	
When under three and over three digits both occur in same sentence		X

Source

Cite the source of your information unless this is your own compilation. The source should be aligned with the right-hand margin of the illustration.

List of Illustration Sources

Most libraries will have all the sources listed below. Note that the examples in these books should be followed in light of the suggestions given previously in this section. Headings and content notes follow the method given in this text rather than that found in the illustrations of the suggested sources. Titles only are given as they are the easiest to locate in a library card catalog.

Most encyclopedia yearbooks, government documents, and dissertations give numerous illustrations. Also general books in statistics, economics, and economic geography supply many illustrations. General computer books will be a source of flow charts and general physical geography books will illustrate a variety of maps.

Computer Yearbook and Directory (annual) Good for flow charts

Statistical Abstracts of the United States (annual)

United States Government Organization Manual (annual) In the back will be found a complete section of various organizational charts.

DIVISION HEADINGS

The main body of a paper will be divided into chapters, i.e., Chapter I, Chapter II, each chapter having a separate title. These chapters may be grouped into related parts as illustrated in the Table of Contents examples in the Preliminary Pages Section. Each chapter may be divided into sections and subsections. The following examples will illustrate relationships and spacing of these various divisions.

Ranks of Headings

The rank of headings is indicated by either all capital letters, underlining, indention, or a combination of two of these. The order of importance is in a descending order:

PARTS (on separate page preceding first chapter of that group)

Chapter I
FORMAL TITLE OF CHAPTER
Centered Heading
Centered Heading
Side Heading
Side Heading
Paragraph side heading.
1.
2.

Any combination of the above headings may be used as long as they are in the order of importance, e.g., you may use only side headings under a chapter heading or just center headings under a chapter. Sample pages follow giving spacing and indention.

Sample Half-title Page

KEY TO RESEARCH

(This half-title page heading, all in capitals, is necessary only for a paper in which chapters are grouped into parts. It is placed immediately before the first chapter of that group. A half-title page is included before the Appendix and Bibliography. Placement of the half-title heading is 1/3 distance of paper from the top. If the title is long, set it in two or more double-spaced lines, in inverted-pyramid form.)

(all half-title pages are centered and numbered at the bottom of the page in Arabic numerals)

46

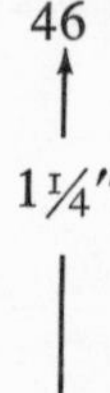

Sample Chapter Page

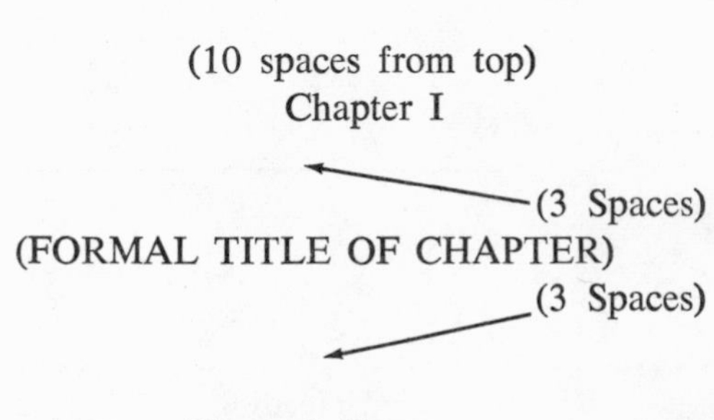

Text of Paper......

(Each chapter must begin on a new page. Capitalize only the first letter of "Chapter." Center the chapter heading in all capital letters. If the title is long, set in two or more double-spaced lines, in inverted-pyramid form.)

DISCUSSION OF ENTRY ARRANGEMENT
BY A.L.A. RULES COMPARED
WITH THE CODE

Keep numeral centered at the bottom of page within bottom margin (1¼″) and two spaces below text.

25

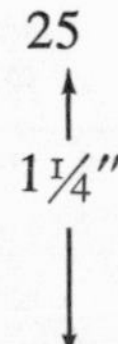

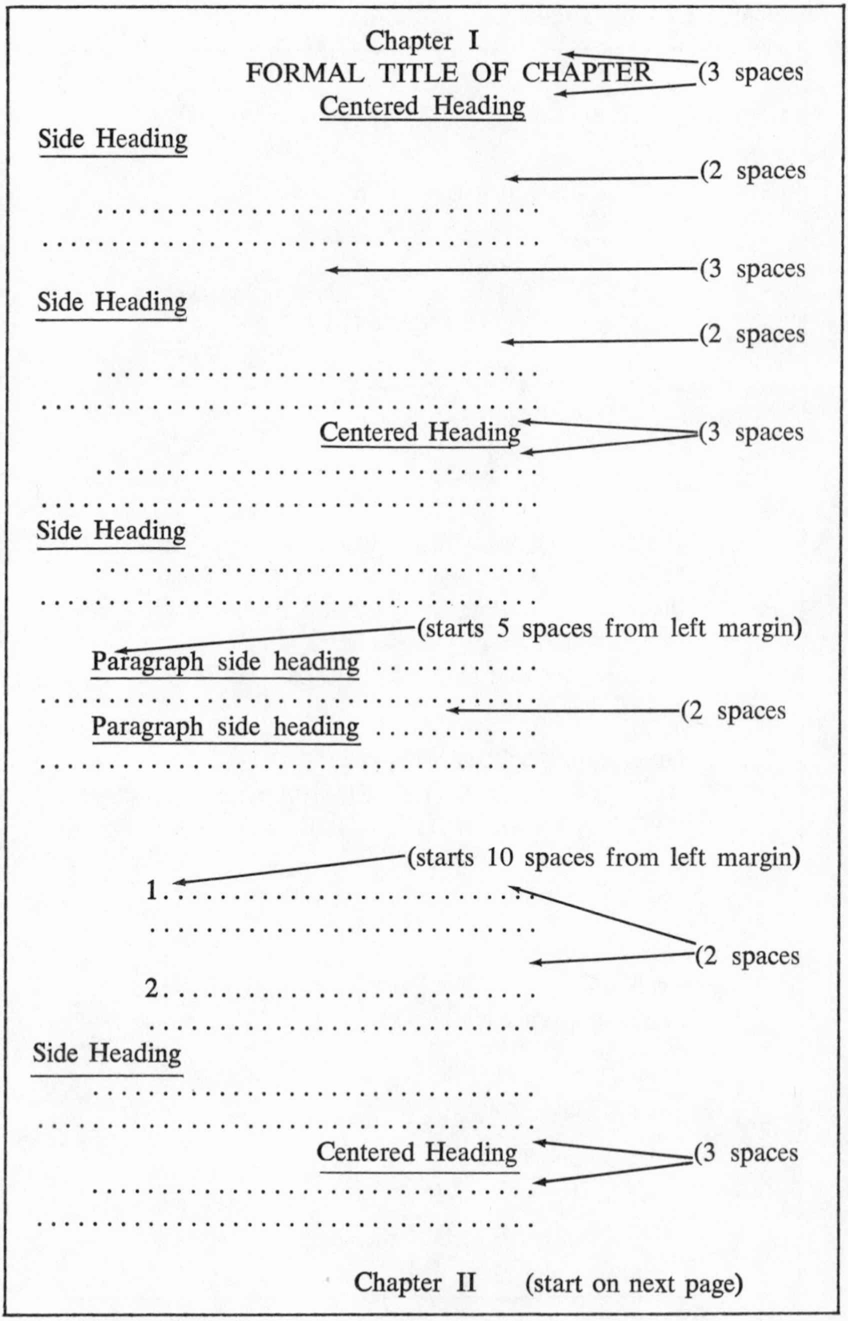

Chapter I

FORMAL TITLE OF CHAPTER (3 spaces

Centered Heading

Side Heading

(2 spaces

. . . .

. . . .

(3 spaces

Side Heading

(2 spaces

. . . .

. . . .

Centered Heading (3 spaces

. . . .

. . . .

Side Heading

. . . .

. . . .

(starts 5 spaces from left margin)

Paragraph side heading . . . .

. . . . (2 spaces

Paragraph side heading . . . .

. . . .

(starts 10 spaces from left margin)

1. . . . .

. . . . (2 spaces

2. . . . .

. . . .

Side Heading

. . . .

. . . .

Centered Heading (3 spaces

. . . .

. . . .

Chapter II (start on next page)

Although centered headings and side headings which are not underlined may be used for less important headings, it is seldom that such headings are necessary. Note in the above example that there is a minimum of two headings at any given level.

Formal Title of Chapter

These headings are triple-spaced above and below. Lengthy headings taking two or more lines should be in the inverted-pyramid format, no line being more than four inches long, single spaced between lines. The title is in full capitals with no end punctuation. An introductory paragraph may be placed between the formal title of the chapter and the first centered heading.

Centered Headings

Triple-space above and below centered headings. Lengthy headings taking two or more lines should be in the inverted-pyramid format, no line being more than four inches long. Single-space between lines. The first letter of major words of the title are capitalized with no end punctuation. Underline the heading.

Side Headings

Triple-space above and double space below side headings. Begin each side heading at the left-hand margin. The first letter of major words of this heading are capitalized with no end punctuation. Underline the heading. If a side heading is more than a half-line in length, divide evenly into two or more single-spaced lines. Indent two spaces on the second line of the heading:

. . . text . . .

←——————— (3 spaces)

Extended Example of Entries
  Filed by the Code

←——————— (2 spaces)

. . . text . . .

Paragraph sidehead

Triple-space above these headings. Only the first word is capitalized. Follow the heading with a period. Continue the text on the same line as heading. Any subpoints are indented five spaces, enumerated by Arabic numerals. The following lines of subpoints are brought back to the left-hand margin in line with the numeral.

WRITING AND PROOFREADING

First Draft

It is advantageous, at this point, to make the outline detailed, for it will greatly aid in the first draft of the paper. With a detailed outline you can write the first draft rapidly, forgetting sentence structure, spelling, style, an so forth. As a general rule, it is better to write too much in the first draft than to write too little, for it is easier to strike superfluous words than to insert omitted ones. The main thing is to get the content before you. In so doing, be sure you provide ample space for alterations, corrections, and additions. This may be accomplished by either using very large margins or wide spaces between lines. Use only one side of the paper except for lengthy additions. Whether you develop the paper as a whole or develop completely one subdivision of your outline at a time makes little difference, for the same general procedure applies in either case.

It is not necessary in the first draft to insert all quotations, tables, and charts. However, indicate in this draft where each insert goes. Quotations on note cards can simply be attached to the first draft in the appropriate places with scotch tape. Illustrative materials can be filed in the approximate places following the first mention of such. All citations and content notes should be listed in the text of the first draft and in all revisions. As will be noted, the method used here of documentation simplifies citation notes and relieves the tedious and non-rewarding task of allowing and adjusting space for traditional footnotes at the bottom of the page. If the content note cards have been filled out as suggested in the Chapter "Recording the Findings," all the information needed will be at hand, and in the exact form to be used.

Getting Started

At the outset give some direction to the reader as to where you are going. The beginning paragraph can accomplish this by incorporating your thesis or purpose. The reader will then want to know how you can prove such. Capturing the readers attention immediately is important. An appropriate and well-worded title to your subject may also arouse interest in what otherwise might sound like a very dull topic.

The Text

This is the exposition of the information collected during research on which thinking is based. Interest begun must be maintained throughout the paper. Make the paper interesting and readable as well as solid and objective. Put as many ideas as possible into your own words and avoid overuse of quotations. Call attention to other opinions and dispose of them as a means of increasing interest in your ideas. Increase the presentation with more interesting facts, progressively substantiate views, or increase authoritative material as you drive toward your conclusion.

Coming to the End

If a formal conclusion is chosen, it is advantageous if it can be connected to the introduction. This ending may be a summary—reviewing major points set forth. The conclusion may be merely a special idea, a conviction reached, or a result. The final comments may forecast or prophesy things to come.

A final point or two should be emphasized concerning the first draft. Keep all note cards until the paper is handed in and returned. It may also be well worth the effort and cost to either make a carbon copy or a photocopy of the first draft. Both the saving of note cards and the extra copy will insure against loss.

You will be more objective re-examining the first draft if you are able to "get away" and do something else for a few days. This helps set the stage for the next section or revision.

Revising and Editing

The chances of achieving the best results on the first draft are remote. The need for several revisions is the average and you might as well resign yourself to this inevitable drudgery. At this point, the paper may be basically a collection of ideas, facts, and statistics. Turn the ideas into effective sentences and paragraphs.

Meaning must be made clear, say what you mean and avoid things not meant. Facts and statistics must come alive; to accomplish this, certain essentials are necessary. A realiable up-date rhetoric handbook and several dictionaries must be at your disposal. Two "musts" are *Roget's International Thesaurus* and *Webster's Dictionary of Synonyms*. Other outstanding aids may be added, such as specialized dictionaries in various fields.

The following check list of questions are concerned primarily with the paper's content and general impressions.

What Was I Trying to Do or Say?

Have I captured the reader at the very beginning?

Have I stated clearly what I intended to do?

Does the paper possess direction?

Is there a single, controlling impression?

Was I Successful?

Did I say what I meant to say?

Have I achieved a balance?

Are my major points adequately presented?

Do I need additional evidence?

Do I need additional analogy or analysis?

Are the facts accurate; check statements and conclusions. Does it require further proof or substantiation?

Are these facts and presentations adequate?

Should anything be eliminated, condensed, or rearranged?

Are all citations of references and sources accurate?

What Is the Paper's Significance?

Does the conclusion tell the reader that the research paper is definitely finished?

Have I convinced myself or anyone else?

Is the significance of my research made clear?

Is this a contribution to knowledge?

What Do Others Think?

What does another think of its general content?

What does another think of its writing mechanics?

Have I Revised and Rewritten Sufficiently?

Have I Read and Reread Sufficiently?

Proofreader Marks

These are symbols or abbreviations used for the purpose of saving time in making corrections. Both writer and typist must understand these marks. The marks are usually indicated in the margin of the paper. These examples represent only the more common proofreader marks.

Mark	Meaning
₰	Delete
₰̂	Delete and close up
⟳	Reverse
⁐	Close up
#	Insert space
⁐/#	Close up and insert space
¶	Paragraph
□	Indent 1 em
[	Move to left
]	Move to right
⊔	Lower
⊓	Raise
∧	Insert marginal addition
V∧	Space evenly
X	Broken letter—used in margin
⊥	Push down space
=	Straighten line
‖	Align type
∧,	Insert comma
∨'	Insert apostrophe
∨"	Insert quotation mark
=/	Insert hyphen
em/	Insert em dash
en/	Insert en dash
∧;	Insert semicolon
⊙:	Insert colon and en quad
⊙	Insert period and en quad
?/	Insert interrogation point
(?)	Query to author—in margin
⌒	Use ligature
(sp)	Spell out
tr	Transpose
wf	Wrong font
bf	Set in **boldface** type
rom	Set in (roman) type
ital	Set in *italic* type
caps	Set in CAPITALS
sc	Set in SMALL CAPITALS
lc	Set in lower case
⁄L	Lower-case letter
stet	Let it stand; restore words crossed out
no ¶	Run in same paragraph
ld in>	Insert lead between lines
hr #	Hair space between letters

Sample Page

The architects of the American Revolution, as distnct
from leaders of the French revolution made no attempt to
carry There plans and and blueprints other into countries or
bayonet edge. wherever the news of their Declaration
rea ched, it was understood that the rights of man on
which they hadstaked their lives were rights not only of
English-men or americans but of men everywhere.
No one could reasonably accuse them of ideological
imperialism. The great continuing principle of the
American Revolution declares that all governments derive
their just powers from the uncovered consent of the
governed What makes these powers just is that they
scure certain rights of men.

Retyped making corrections

The architects of the American Revolution, as distinct from leaders of the French Revolution, made no attempt to carry there plans and blueprints into other countries or bayonet edge. Wherever the news of their Declaration reached, it was understood that the rights of man on which they had staked their lives were rights not only of English-men or Americans but of men everywhere. No one could reasonably accuse them of ideological imperialism.

The great continuing principle of the American Revolution declares that all governments derive their just powers from the uncovered consent of the governed. What makes these powers just is that they secure certain rights of men.

Supplementary Pages

APPENDIXES

A half-title appendix page is included before the appendix text in a formal paper.

The first page of the appendix is headed:

Appendix (7-10 spaces from top of page)

or

Appendix I (if more than one appendix)

If the appendix covers a specific type of material, i.e., sample pages, glossary, abbreviations, etc., indicate such immediately under "Appendix" and in full capitals.

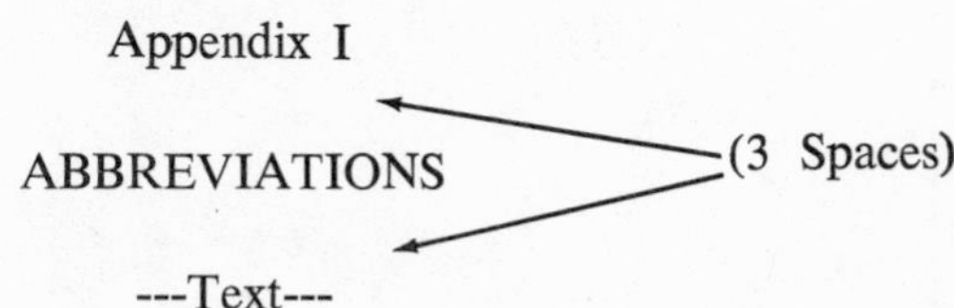

Each type of appendix should begin on a new page. If there is an insufficient top margin for a heading (when material fills the page completely, such as a map or chart) precede this page with a half-title page. If this change is needed for one type of appendix, follow the same throughout. Again, BE CONSISTENT.

Because of the variety of material which may be placed in appendixes, the most we can suggest is that consistency be followed wherever possible.

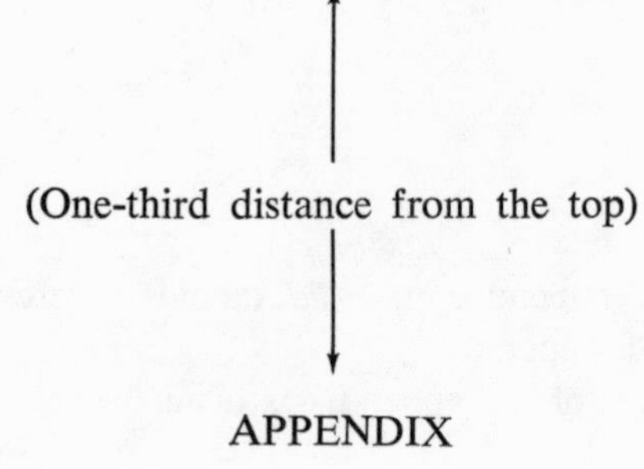

APPENDIX

(This half-title page precedes the appendix text,
but is not needed for a brief paper.
The title is in full capitals.)

(Number this page centered at the bottom.)

146

1¼″

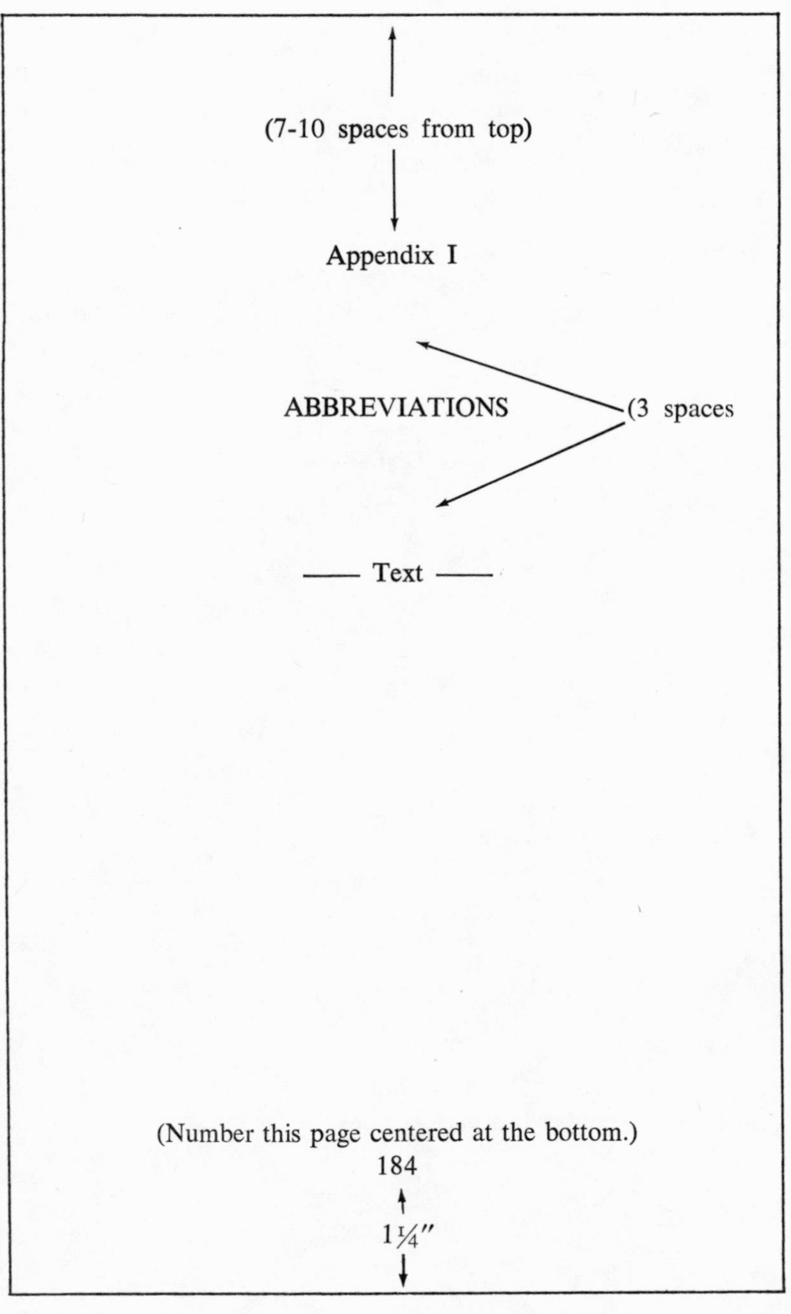
(7-10 spaces from top)
Appendix I
ABBREVIATIONS
(3 spaces
Text
(Number this page centered at the bottom.)
184
1¼″

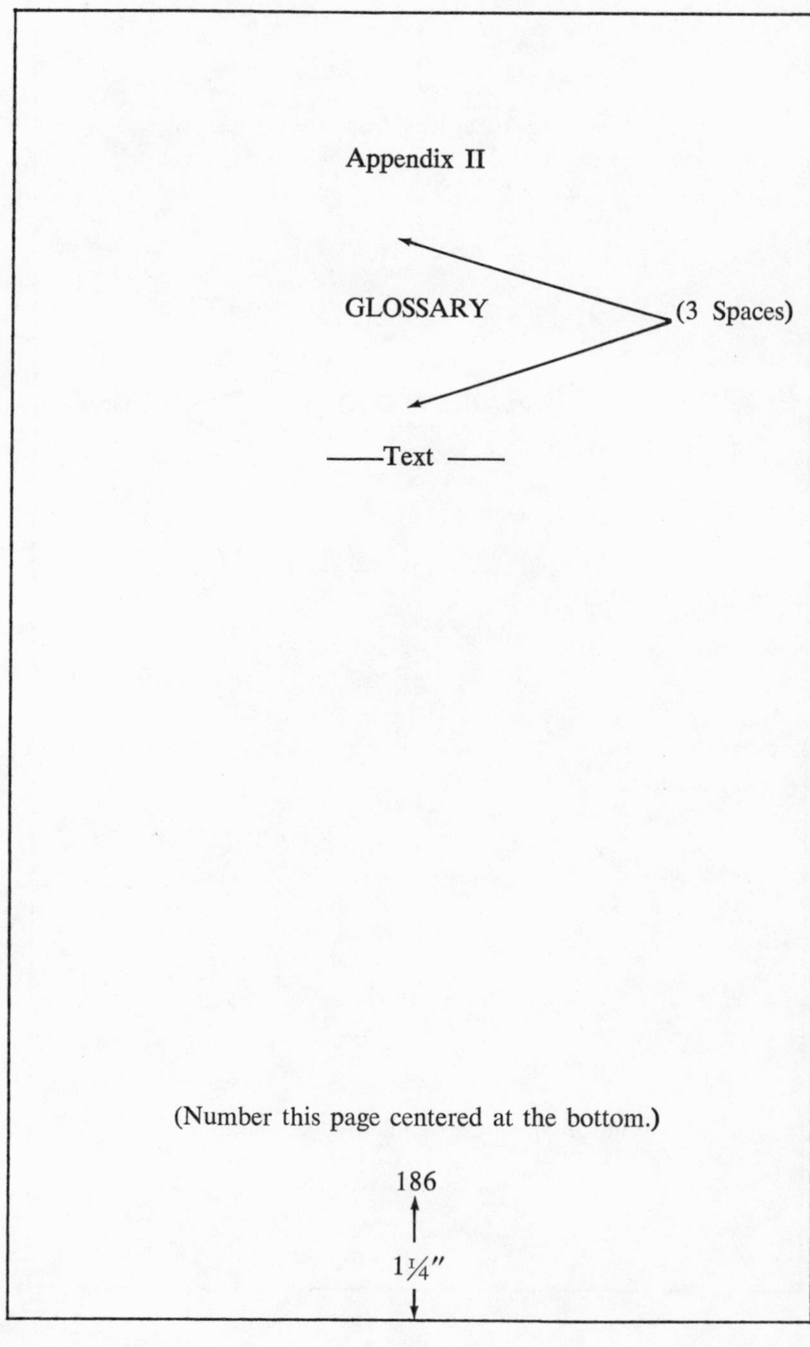

Appendix II
GLOSSARY
(3 Spaces)
—Text —
(Number this page centered at the bottom.)
186
1¼″

BIBLIOGRAPHY

Documentation need not be tedious, irksome, or exasperating. Described herein is a simplified bibliography entry with a clear format, providing all neccesary information in eight divisions. A wide variety of materials used in a research paper, such as books, periodicals, manuscripts, government documents, can be readily and uniformly adapted to the eight basic divisions outlined under bibliography. These eight divisions illustrate the possible parts of a bibliography entry-one can simply exclude a division not applicable, and go on to the next sequence.

HERE, ALL TYPES OF SOURCE MATERIALS (BOOKS, PERIODICALS, LETTERS, AND SO FORTH) CONFORM TO THE SAME BASIC ORDER. There is no need in this method, as required in other guides to compiling bibliographies, to require several forms of entry, depending on the type of material used. There is only one order and form to learn for all sources, thus simplifying the mechanics of documentation. Basic information including the general format and the bibliography entry are first discussed, followed by a detailed description of each part, and special bibliography problems. In most cases the basic information in the next few pages may suffice both beginner and advanced student for all bibliography needs.

Bibliography Formats

The bibliography must include all references listed in the text of the paper, as well as other relevant materials consulted while preparing the research paper. A half-title page with the word "BIBLIOGRAPHY" precedes the bibliography text. The first page of the bibliography text is headed:

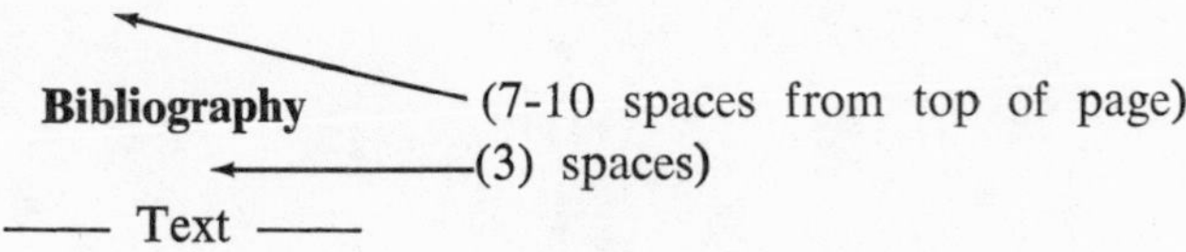

The bibliography may be divided into a variety of sections. Label it precisely, e.g., "A Selected Bibliography," "A Brief Annotated Bibliography," or "Primary Sources," etc. See Appendix II for a complete sample bibliography.

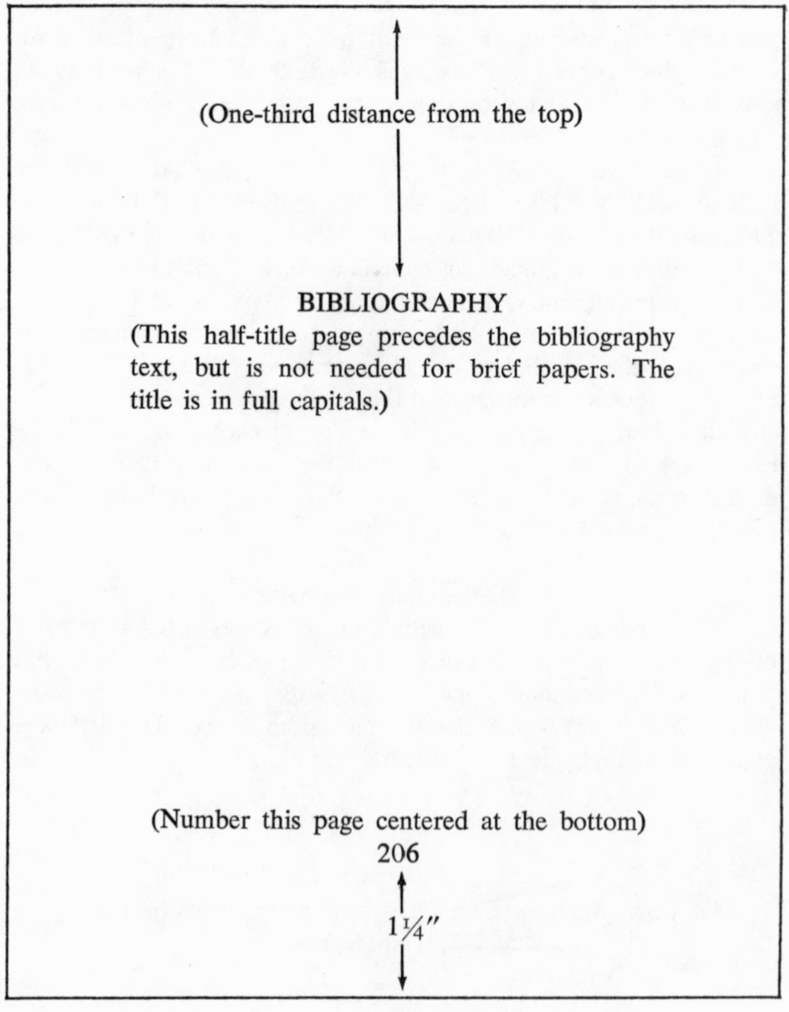

(One-third distance from the top)
BIBLIOGRAPHY
(This half-title page precedes the bibliography text, but is not needed for brief papers. The title is in full capitals.)
(Number this page centered at the bottom)
206
1¼″

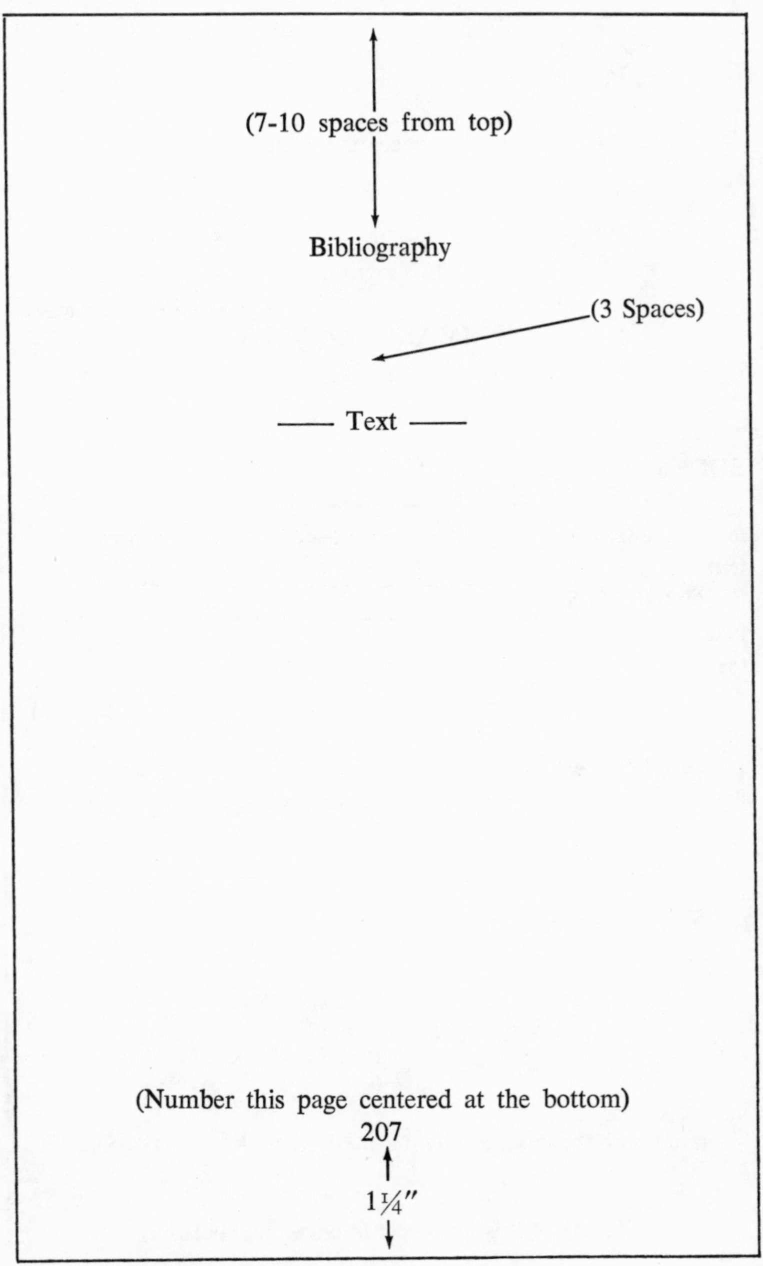
(7-10 spaces from top)
Bibliography
(3 Spaces)
—— Text ——
(Number this page centered at the bottom)
207
1¼″

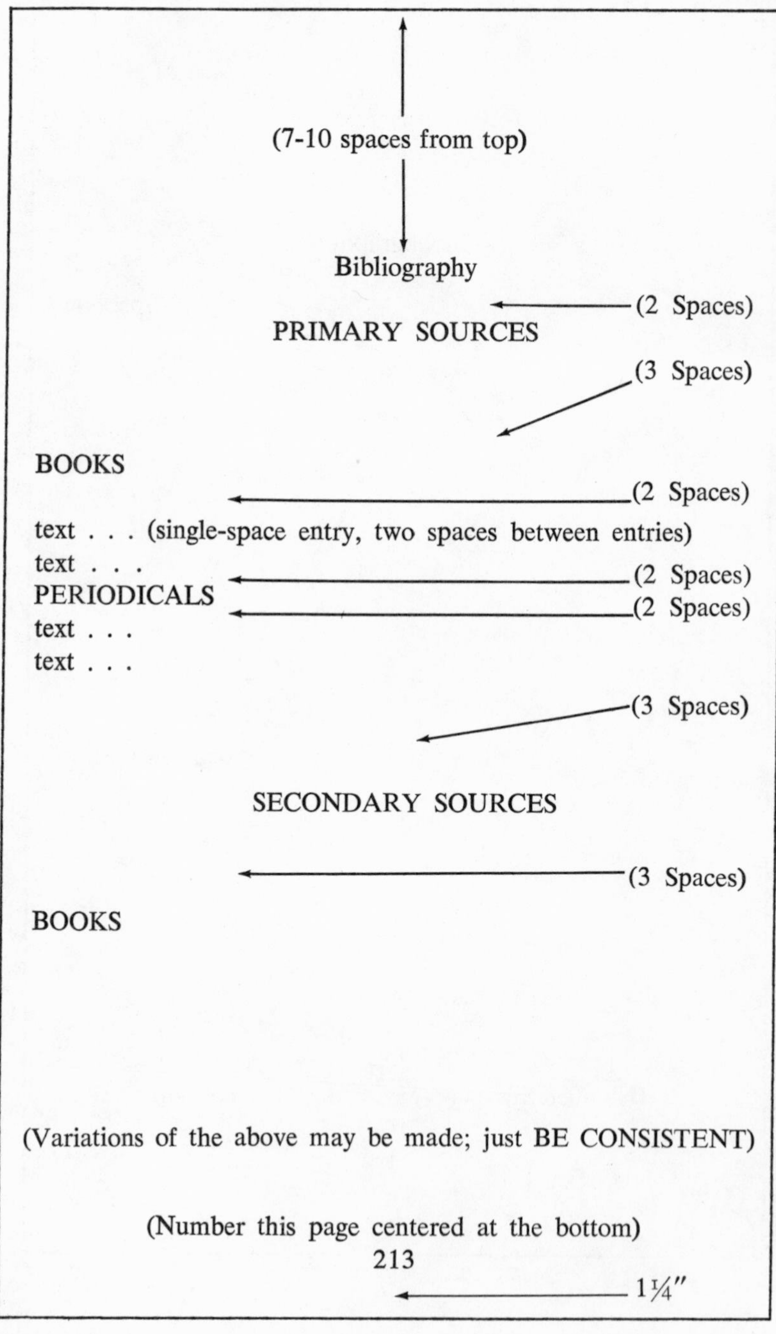
(7-10 spaces from top)
Bibliography
(2 Spaces)
PRIMARY SOURCES
(3 Spaces)
BOOKS
(2 Spaces)
text . . . (single-space entry, two spaces between entries)
text . . .
(2 Spaces)
PERIODICALS
(2 Spaces)
text . . .
text . . .
(3 Spaces)
SECONDARY SOURCES
(3 Spaces)
BOOKS
(Variations of the above may be made; just BE CONSISTENT)
(Number this page centered at the bottom)
213
1¼″

The Bibliography Entry

A good bibliography meets these qualifications: (1) completeness of your source, (2) uniformity of sequence, (3) and enough flexibility to make possible the inclusion of complex information in a consistent manner. The following points illustrate these essentials of the bibliographic entry. SEE ALSO pp. 30-31.

Sample Bibliography Entry

BOOK: This example represents the most common book entry.

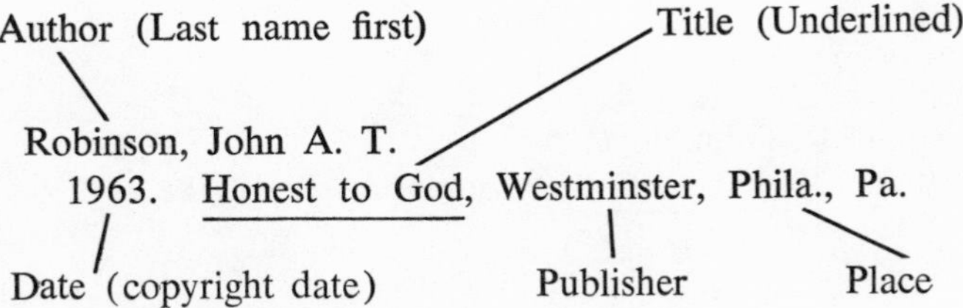

PERIODICAL: This example represents a typical periodical entry.

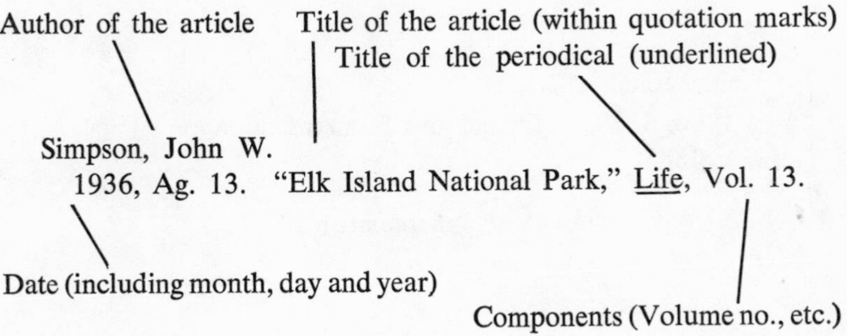

Basic Order of Sequence

Summary of the basic order of sequence for the bibliography entry are Author, Date, Title, Initiator, Special Note, Components, Publisher and Place, and if desired, an eighth division, of total or inclusive pages. Examples (arrows) illustrate each specific point:

AUTHOR—the person or corporate body chiefly responsible for creation of the content of the book or article. As used here, authors include editor and compiler, with the exception indicated under point 4 below. The author's last name is given first and in the fullest form known to you.

Robinson, John A. T. ←
1963. Honest to God, Westminster, Phila., Pa.

DATE—the copyright date is more dependable and of greater significance than the printing date.

Book:

Robinson, John A. T.
→1963. Honest to God, Westminster, Phila., Pa.

Periodical:

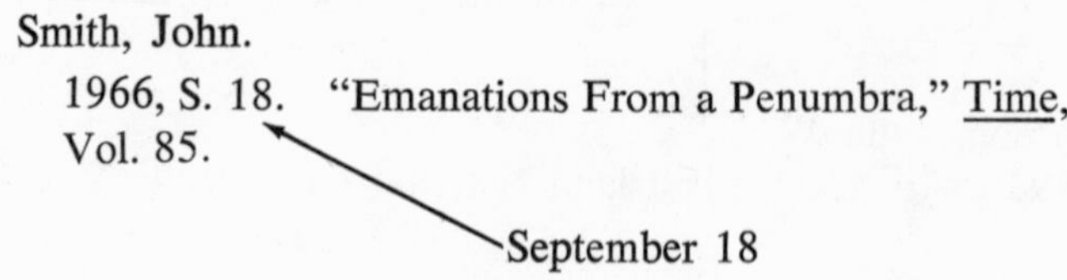
Smith, John.
1966, S. 18. "Emanations From a Penumbra," Time, Vol. 85.

TITLE—the distinguishing name.
Primary title (the specific title referred to)

Book:

Robinson, John A. T.
1963. Honest to God, Westminster, Phila., Pa.

Periodical:

Smith, John.
1966, S. 18. "Emanations From a Penumbra," Time, Vol. 85.

Secondary title, if needed (subordinate, yet requisite; it is the inclusive title)

Book:

Lusby, Frederick Stanley.
1966. "Ancestor Worship," Encyclopedia Britannica, Vol. 1, Encyclopaedia Britannica, Chicago, Ill.

Periodical:

Smith, John.
1966, S. 18. "Emanations From a Penumbra," Time, Vol. 85.

INITIATOR—the person(s) responsible for initiating the work (not the creator of the content), i.e., translator, compiler, or editor. Give the name in normal order.

Editor of a Book:

Brown, Bob C.
1943. "The Way to Town," A Collection of Essays, ed. by John B. Hines, Harper, N. Y.

Translator of a Book:

Harris, John B.
1965. The Man From Bro-Dart, tr. by H. L. Smith, Random, N. Y.

SPECIAL NOTE—other information useful or necessary for clarification or identification. This information is enclosed within parentheses.

A book which is part of a series:

Hirschman, Albert O.
1958. The Strategy of Economic Development. (Yale Studies in Economics, No. 10) Yale U., New Haven, Conn.

Useful Information about the material cited:

Hall, Fred P.
1957. Poems of Freedom. (Unpublished manuscript) Buffalo, N. Y.

COMPONENTS—the distinctive units of the material, i.e., volumes parts, edition, sections, etc. Abbreviate when possible.

Commager, Henry Steele, ed.
1963. Documents of American History, 7th ed., Appleton, N. Y.

Boyet, W. E. November

1966, N. "Recreation Projection on Demand Analysis," Journal of Farm Economics, Vol. 48, No. 4, pt. 1.

PUBLISHER AND PLACE—the name and location of the press responsible for issuing the material. This information is not given for Periodicals. Abbreviate when possible, put preserve clarity.

Dillard, Dudely.
1948. The Economics of John Maynard Keynes, Prentice-Hall, Englewood Cliffs, N. J.

PAGE OPTION—give the inclusive pages or total number of pages if required.

Books total pages:

Baillie, John.
1959. Our Knowledge of God, Scribner's, N. Y. 263 pp.

Periodical inclusive pages:

Simpson, George W.
1936. "Elk Island National Park," Life, Vol. 13, pp. 23-37.

It must be remembered that these eight divisions represent the most complete entry possible. Any one division may be excluded if not applicable; in that case, proceed to the next division in sequence. See Appendix II for an extensive sample bibliography.

Form and Punctuation of Bibliography

The bibliography entry will be similar to the following model:

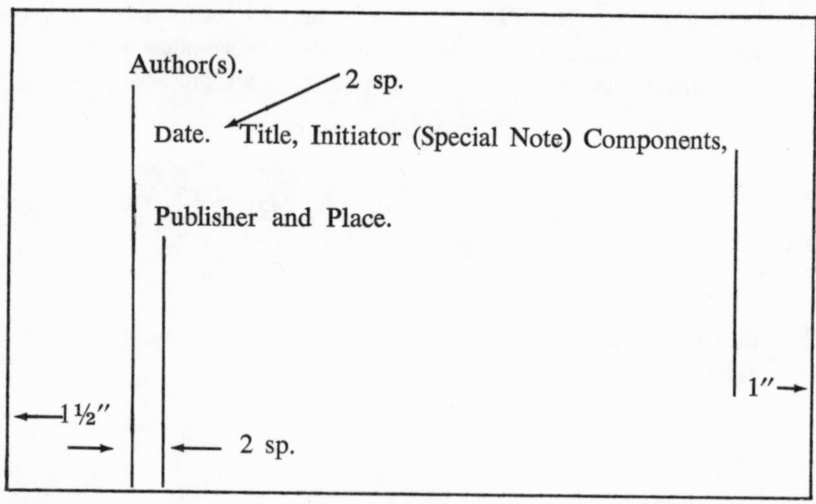

1. Each entry is listed alphabetically by the author's last name.
2. The author's name is in alignment with the left-hand margin (1½″ in from left-hand edge of paper.)
3. Indent the second line of the entry two spaces. Align additional lines of the same entry with the second line.
4. Leave 2 spaces between the date period and the title.
5. A period follows the author's name, date, and at end of the entry.
6. A comma follows all other divisions of the entry, except when parentheses are used.
7. When not listing a "Special Note," insert a comma after the "Initiator." No comma before or following parentheses.
8. Single-space each entry, double-space between entries.

Detailed Description of Bibliography Parts

Each of the eight basic divisions of a bibliographic entry is described in detail and illustrated below.

AUTHOR(S) (Begin at lefthand margin)

An author is the name of the corporate body or person(s) chiefly responsible for creation of the content of the work or for presenting the material (information) in this form. As used here, authors include editors(s) and compiler(s), with the exception indicated under the INITIATOR below. An author may be an:

Institution
Government, various units of, i.e., City, State, etc.
Organization or Society
Legislative body
Business firm
Individual

The surname of an individual is always listed first, followed by a comma, then the given name. Names given within the entry are given in their normal order, i.e., Emerson E. Dunn. Always give the fullest form of the name known, followed by a period. The full name will usually be given in the library card catalog in which the material is found.

More than one name given: If only two names, give in order as they appear on the title page, e.g., Dunn, Emerson A. and East, Palmer W. When more than two names are given, list the first name, then add "and others," e.g., Elton, Durrant S. and others.

Anonymous: When a name is withheld or unknown, simply list this entry separately in the bibliography following the author listings, chronologically-earliest date first, then alphabetically by title. If the correct name of the author is supplied, enclose it with square brackets: [More, Frank E.] Whenever an author's name is supplied, the entry should be placed among the alphabetical author list in the bibliography. Note that catalog card may give author, though it is not found in the book. Examples of anonymous entries:

> 1965, Je. 18. "Emanations from a Penumbra," <u>Time</u>, Vol. 63.
> 1966, Ag. 10. "Politics of Freedom," <u>The Cleveland Plain Dealer</u>.

Also include in the nonauthor listing encyclopedias and other general reference books known primarily by their titles.

1966. McGraw-Hill Encyclopedia of Science and Technology, Vol. 13, McGraw-Hill, N. Y.

1966. "Trebonius, Gaius," Encyclopaedia Britannica, Vol. 22, Encyclopaedia Britannica, Chicago, Ill.

1967. Encyclopedia of Chemical Technology, Vol. 12, 2d ed., Interscience, N. Y.

It is not necessary to give the names of the editors of general encyclopedias or other reference works known primarily by their titles.

Pseudonymous author: If pseudonymity is indicated on the title page, list it as:

Twain, Mark, pseud.

If pseudonymity is not indicated on the title page, but it is an established fact, place the word "pseudonym" (abbreviated) in square brackets after the name:

Twain, Mark [pseud.]

If you supply the real name, enclose the pseudonym with parentheses following the author's real name:

Clemens, Samuel Langhorne (Twain, Mark, pseud.)

When you supply the real name, always make a cross reference in the bibliography from the pseudonym to the real name:

Twain, Mark SEE Clemens, Samuel Langhorne

Do not use titles: Titles such as Dr., Prof., Gen., Msgr., Ph.D., S. J., Pres., etc. are not used unless inclusion is of special significance for the subject under discussion, or to prevent confusion through lack of information.

Jr. after name: If the abbreviation Jr. (junior) follows an author's name, list in the bibliography in the following order:

Williams, Joe B., Jr.

Oriental names: When the author has a Chinese, or certain other Oriental name, check the library card catalog where the material is located and use it as your guide for proper form.

Lengthy authors: Some corporate authors will use more than one line. The second line should be indented two spaces:

West Virginia. Dept. of Employment Security
  Research and Statistics Division.
  1962. Statistical Handbook, Charleston, W. Va.

Lengthy authors need not be listed in the citation note fully written out—just abbreviate.

DATE (indent 2 spaces under author)

The copyright date (when given) is always preferred over the publisher's date or reprint date. The copyright date is located on the page following the title page.

Periodicals, letters, interviews, etc.: Add after the year the month (abbreviated) and day. See standard abbreviations for months in the appendix. Note that the period follows the complete date, a comma being placed after the year when month is given.

1966, Mr. 21. 1954, Ap. 3. 1918, Ag. 5. 1945, Jl.

Sets (completed): Give the inclusive dates.

1962-65. 1966-68.

Sets (incomplete): If the publication of the set is still in progress

1966- 1968-

a period need not follow the dash.

No date: Use "n.d." when no date is given.

Smith, Web. S.
  n.d. The American College, Singer, Kan.

Date supplied: When a date is supplied from another source (other than the book, etc., itself) place it within square brackets:

[1966] [1914]

The complete date is followed by a period: Unless it is enclosed with brackets or followed by a dash.

1914. [1964] 1967— 1966, Ap. 5.

Date uncertain: If a date cannot be ascertained, a date is supplied as follows:

probable date	[1875?]
decade certain	[188-]
decade uncertain	[179-?]
century certain	[17-]

Bibliography arrangement: The usual arrangement is first by author, then by date, followed by title. The date sequence is from earliest to latest.

1913
1956
1969
1969a

The general year date precedes all specific dates of the same year. Those specific dates follow in order of the calendar month and day:

1966
1966a.
1966, S.
1966, S. 23.

TITLE (2 spaces following date)

The title is the distinguishing name of the book, periodical, newspaper, article, etc. The distinguishing characteristics of titles, as used here, are discussed below.

Primary title: This directs one to the specific title of the book or part of a book or periodical (poem, essay, article, etc.) to which you are referring. Normally you should never refer to an anthology of essays as a whole. Therefore, when using material from Frederick

Stanley Lusby's article, "Ancestor Worship," found in the Encyclopaedia Britannica, it is not the Encyclopaedia Britannica that is of "primary" importance for citing in a note or listing in the bibliography; it is Frederick Lusby and his article. Thus, when citing this source in the bibliography, the "primary" author and title are listed first:

Primary title

Lusby, Frederick Stanley.
1966. "Ancestor Worship," Encyclopaedia Britannica, Vol. 1, Encyclopaedia Britannica, Chicago, Ill.

Similarly, this same rule is followed when an article is used from a periodical:

Primary title

Okamoto, T.
1966, S. "On the Keynesian Theory of Distribution," Bulletin of the University of Osaka Prefecture, Vol. 10, ser. D.

In referring to the entire book, the overall title is the "primary" title:

Brown, Bob C.
1961. Ancestor Worship in the U. S., Harper, N. Y.

Secondary title: It is the inclusive title of a collected work of essays, poems, etc., or the name of the periodical:

Secondary title

Brown, Smith P.
1968. "The Way Back," To the Moon, ed. by Ken B. Jordan, 2d ed., Lamb, N. J.

Secondary title
↓

Simpson, George W.
1936, Ag. 13. "Elk Island National Park," Life, Vol. 13.

Punctuation and capitalization of title: Enclose the title of an article, essay, etc., in quotation marks, followed by a comma within the quotation marks.

Singer, Bob B.
1964. "The Way Out," A Collection of Essays, ed. by Sheppard P. Hines, 2d ed., Harper, N. Y.

Underline the overall title of the book or periodical, followed by a comma unless the title is followed by a parenthesis.

Capitalize the first and last words, nouns, pronouns, adjectives, adverbs, and verbs of every title.

Unusually long titles: If the entry has an unusually long title, cut in a convenient place and substitute the omission with an ellipsis.

The Positive Thinkers, a Study of the American Quest for Health, Wealth, and Personal Power from Mary Baker Eddy to Norman Vincent Peale.

This long title may be cut at the first punctuation mark:

The Positive Thinkers . . ..

The title may also be broken in more than one place, i.e.,

Brief Summary of Major Provisions of and Detailed Comparison Showing Changes Made in Existing Law by H. R. 6675 as Passed by the House of Representatives.

This may be changed to:

Brief Summary of . . . in Existing Law by H. R. 6675 . . ..

As a rule of thumb, a title becomes too long when it exceeds eight words. Normally exclude subtitles unless they are necessary to clarify the title.

INITIATOR

The initiator is the person(s) responsible for initiating the publication (not the creator of the content). Many works of multiple authorship are produced under the direction of an editor, or are collections of previously existing works by different authors, compiled by an individual. Another "initiator" may be the translator of a specific author's work. In all three cases, the editor, compiler, or translator is of only secondary importance to the individual author within the work—or the original author in the case of a translation. Whenever citing, the creator of the work takes precedence and is listed first in the entry. The "initiator" is listed immediately after the title:

Brown, Bob C.
1943. "The Way to Town," A Collection of Essays, ed. by John B. Hines, Harper, N. Y.

Green, Richard A.
1926. "Thoughts on Andrew Johnson." Essays on Green, comp. by Paul Owen, Lake, Mich.

Harris, John B.
1965. The Man From Bro-Dart, tr. by H. L. Smith, Random, N. Y.

Follow the name of the translator, compiler, or editor with a comma, unless it is followed by a parenthesis. Editors of periodicals and general encyclopedias are never listed in an entry.

SPECIAL NOTE

This is a sort of catchall to take care of miscellaneous information which may be important. Discretion should dictate its use and limitations. All materials here are placed within parentheses. Several examples of special notes are given below:

Series note:

Hirschman, Albert O.
1958. The Strategy of Economic Development (Yale Studies in Economics, No. 10) Yale U., New Haven, Conn.

The series title is also underlined, and further information as to the number, volume, etc., may be given if useful.

Unpublished manuscript:

Hall, Fred P.
1957. Poems of Freedom (unpublished manuscript) Buffalo, N. Y.

Privately printed:

Barrow, Edward.
1967. A History of Bibliography (privately printed) Edward Barrow, 12 W. 9th St., Chicago, Ill.

Letter:

Jordan, Ben.
1912, Ap. 12. Letter (to Mrs. Mary Smith) Johnson Library, Cleveland, Ohio.

Citation of a letter must always list to whom it was written.

Secondary citation source: This is used when one wishes to quote a source found quoted in another work. Although quoting original sources is always preferred, if one is unable to locate or to have access to the original source, the following is acceptable:

Doyle, Lauren B.
1961, O. "Semantic Road Maps for Literature Searchers," Journal of the Association for Computing Machinery (cited in: Becker, Joseph. 1963. Information Storage and Retrieval, Wiley, N. Y., p. 251) Vol. 8, no. 4.

All information about the secondary source is included in the "special note," including the page where the quotation is found. This information is given in the same order as in a normal entry. The original source is listed first in the bibliographic entry.

Clarification or additional information: Clarification or additional information may include most anything relevant, especially when the title page (of government documents in particular) is confusing as to authorship.

U. S. Library of Congress. General Reference and Bibliography Division.
1960. A Guide to the Study of the United States of Amer-

ica (prepared under the direction of Roy P. Basler and others) U. S. Govt. Print. Off., Wash., D. C.

COMPONENTS

The distinguishing characteristics of materials are listed below:

Volume(s) number (followed by a comma): If the material used consists of more than one volume (a set or volume numbered series), give the specific volume(s) used, i.e., Vols. 3, 9; Vol. 5; 2 vols. Use Arabic numerals. Capitalize as in the examples given.

Parts (followed by a comma unless it is the last part of the entry):

Supplements to sets or volumes:
- Suppl. 1,
- Vol. 2, suppl. 1,
- Vol. 2, suppl. 2.

Parts of sets or volumes:
- Vol. 1, pt. 1,
- Vol. 2, pt. 2,

Series:
- Ser. D,
- 2d. ser.,

Number:
- No. 4, pt. 1,
- No. 22,

Session:
- 2d ses.,
- 4th ses.,

Circular:
- Cir. 712,
- Cir. 91,

Section:
- Sec. 1485,
- Sec. 193,

Article:
- Art. 3,
- Art. 2, sec. 3,

Bulletin:
- Bul. no. 22,
- Bul. no. 3,

Title:
- Title 10,
- Title 98,

Report:

Rep. no. 765,

Rep. no. 3,

Always arrange the parts in order from the largest (the more inclusive) to the smallest. The first letter only is always capitalized of the largest part, or the one listed first.

Editions (followed by a comma): The edition indicates how often a book has been revised, and is usually located on reverse side of title plate. Normally you will use the latest edition of a work, or give justification for using an earlier edition. Earlier editions may be useful to demonstrate an author's change of viewpoint. Representative types of editions are: 2d ed., 3d ed., 4th ed., Rev. ed., Rev. and enl. ed.

Plays (followed by a comma): When referring to specific scenes or acts:

Act. 1,

Act. 2, sc. 1,

Poetry (followed by a comma): When referring to specific stanzas or verses:

St. no. 2,

St. no. 3, v. 2,

V. 3

Order of components: Volume(s), Parts (including Plays and Poetry), and then Edition.

PUBLISHER AND PLACE (followed by a period)

The publisher and place are usually found on the title page. If more than one publisher and/or place are listed, use only the first one listed. If no publisher is listed, put "n.p." (no publisher) in its place.

Crisler, Joel.
1968. The Third Knowledge, n.p.

When neither a publisher nor a place is listed, but there exists a statement "compiled for" or "available from," list such within parentheses.

Smith, Paul.
1963. Documents of Peace, n.p. (available from Chautauque County Court House, Dayton, Ohio)

Note that there is no need for listing the publisher or place for a periodical. Shorten and/or abbreviate well-known publishers and all states. In other words, condense as much as possible without loss of intelligibility or identification.

Omit the following unnecessary parts of the publisher statement:

a). "published by," "published for," or the word "publisher."
b). initial article, i.e., a, an, the.
c). "and Company," "and Sons," etc.
d). terms meaning "Limited" or "Incorporated."

OPTION

The publisher and place may be followed with one or more of the suggestions given below if required by one's instructor.

Annotation: A brief note describing the nature and content of the work.

Hutchinson, David P.
1947. America's Past, Scribner's, N. Y.
A grass-roots approach to causes and trends which throws light upon many lesser-known historians and on the development of several historical societies.

Notice that the annotation is indented two spaces under the date, and single-spaced.

Pages: This may consist of the total number of pages of an article or book.

Baillie, John.
1959. Our Knowledge of God, Scribner's, N. Y., 263 pp.
Hutchinson, David P.
1947. America's Past, Scribner's, N. Y., 233 pp.
Simpson, George W.
1936. "Elk Island National Park," Life, Vol. 13, pp. 23-27.

The pages follow the publisher and place. Cite the page numbers as pp. 556-559, pp. 56-58, pp. 432-428; not as pp. 556-59, pp. 56-8, pp. 423-28. In the case of a book the total listed pages is given, e.g., 224 pp. In the case the material is not numbered, count pages and give this number in brackets [38].

As an alternate to the above, the pages given (in the same location) could refer to the pages used in your paper where this particular material is used.

If no specific reference is cited within the paper for that entry, no pages need be listed. The latter choice helps the reader to understand and evaluate the writer's use of this material. Whichever use is made of pages throughout the bibliography should be noted at the foot of the first page of the bibliography.

Primary or secondary sources: The type of source may be indicated as the final item of an entry, or the entire bibliography may be divided into separate divisions by types of sources. See sample Bibliography II for an example of separate divisions by types.

Edition: Explanation of the reason for not using the latest edition:

Hunt, Paul S.
  1926. Knowledge of the U. S., 2d ed., Harper, N. Y.
    The 3d ed. was not available in libraries located in this area.

Indent note two spaces under the date and single-space.

Special Bibliography Problems

The following examples illustrate bibliography entries and citation notes for various special problem sources.

Book Reviews

The order of entry is:

1. Name of the reviewer
2. Date of the publication where the review is found
3. Title of the book reviewed in quotation marks
4. Title of the source—periodical, book, etc,
5. Special note—author of the book reviewed
6. Components
7. Publisher and place if the review is taken from a book (unnecessary for periodicals or newspapers)

Reviewer named:

Pickrel, Paul, reviewer.

1967, S. "All the Little Live Things," Harpers Magazine (by Wallace Stegner) Vol. 235, No. 1408.

Citation note: (Pickrel, 1967, 118)

Reviewer's initials given:

T. D., reviewer.

1967, D. "Modern Egypt," Current History (by Tom Little) Vol. 53, No. 316.

Citation note: (T. D., 1967, 359)

Reviewer's name or initials not given:

Reviewer.

1968, Ja. "A Critical Approach to Children's Literature," Choice (by James Steel Smith) Vol. 4, No. 11.

Citation note: (Reviewer, 1968, 1237)

Classical Works

Enter classical works in the bibliography just as you would other materials. In other words, all facts of publication are included.

Legal Materials

These comments are intended for the infrequent user of legal materials. Consult A Uniform System of Citation, 11th ed., 1967, The Harvard Law Review Association, for papers that are predominantly legal.

Rather than attempt to give all the complexities in this field, only those thought to be most useful to the non-law student are given. Traditionally, the entry of legal materials is very condensed, using abbreviations whenever possible. However, for the infrequent user, it is suggested to err in giving too much information, and to limit abbreviations to the obvious. The attempt here is to preserve a uniform style by means of this book, yet cause little confusion for those familiar with the standard form as given in A Uniform System of Citation.

The general order of the entry is as follows;

1. Name of case (in the author place). The plaintiff is mentioned first followed by the defendant.

2. Date of publication. If decision date differs from the publication date, the decision date is given in the special note.

3. Title or name of law report(s) or journal.
4. Initiator—Court reporter, if given.
5. Special note includes jurisdiction, decision date, etc.
6. Components—Volumes, sections, and beginning page of the case.
7. Publisher and place are normally not given. However, if this information will clarify entry, state such.

(Example a)

Clagett v. Daly.
1966. Supreme Court Reporter, Vol. 87, 311*.

*Only the first page is given in court cases.

Citation note: (Clagett v. Daly, 1966, 311)

(Example b)

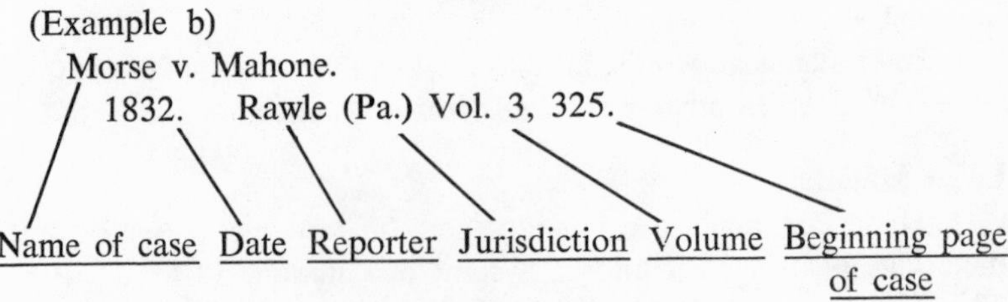

Citation note: (Morse v. Mahone, 1832, 325)

General rules to observe with legal material:

1. When referring to a court case as a whole, only the number of the first page is listed.
2. When a reference is made to a specific point within a case, the number of the first page and that containing the cited material, separated by a comma, is given, i.e., 385, 389.
3. Although abbreviations may be used with discretion in the entry, the word is spelled out in all textual matter, other than the citation note.
4. Indicate in the entry the court that decided the case.
5. Inasmuch as each series for English court cases is renumbered yearly, both the publication date and volume number are necessary.

6. Most abbreviations used in legal entries will be found in A Uniform System of Citation. You may need this to interpret information found in other sources.
7. The plaintiff is mentioned first, followed by the defendant.

Comber v. Jones

Plaintiff—the one who sues.

Defendant—the party sued.

8. In older works, (before 1875) a "reporter" or "report editor" is often mentioned. This "reporter's" last name follows the date or title (if given).
9. Both the jurisdiction and the name of the court must be added to the special note. However, if the court that rendered the decision is the highest of the jurisdiction, only the jurisdiction need be mentioned.
10. Indicate the circuit number when referring to a case decided by a U. S. court of appeals.
11. Legal reports and statutes are usually uncopyrighted public property and may be quoted freely. If, however, these reports or statutes are quoted from a secondary source, permission for lengthy quotes must be obtained from the secondary source, and credit given to that source.

Letters and Interviews

The name of the person who wrote the letter or who was interviewed is given as the author, and the place where the letter originated or the interview took place is recorded in place of the publisher.

Personal letters or interview: A letter or interview written or spoken directly to you is entered as follows:

Johnson, Lewis E.
1966, Jl. 2. Personal Letter, Chicago, Ill.

Citation note: (Johnson, 1966)

Smith, John P.
1964, D. 3. Personal Interview, New York, N. Y.

Citation note: (Smith, 1964)

Specific event: If the interview is associated with a specific event, state such in the special note:

Anderson, Ben.
1966, Jl. 11. Personal Interview (American Library Association Convention) New York, N. Y.

Citation note: (Anderson, 1966)

Letter from an unpublished collection: If the letter(s) are a part of an unpublished collection, include the name of the person to whom the letter was addressed, and the name of the library or other source and place:

Jordan, Ben.
1912. Ap. 12. Letter (to Mrs. Mary Smith) Johnson Library, Cleveland, Ohio.

Citation note: (Jordan, 1912)

Letters which are a part of a published work:

Lincoln, Abraham.
1863, Jl. 6. "Letter to Henry W. Halleck," The Collected Works of Abraham Lincoln, ed. by Roy P. Basler, Vol. 6, Rutgers U., New Brunswick, N. J.

Citation note: (Lincoln, 1863)

Manuscript Collections

Treat as letters or similar material. Always give the location, title, number, or similar designation to aid the reader in locating the material.

Microfilm

All materials, books, periodicals, etc., on microfilm may be entered into the bibliography in the same manner as a bound book or periodical. If judged important to mention that the material is on microfilm, it should be indicated as such in the special note.

Public Documents

Public documents are among the most frustrating research materials to cite and enter in a bibliography. Their wealth of information is undeniable; their use in research may be unavoidable; and their complexities, when it comes to citing, may seem intolerable. Perhaps this explains the primary reason most guides to documentation avoid mention of public documents altogether, or give only a few examples which never seem to "fit" one particular case.

The typical title page of most books follows a traditional arrangement or format, giving the title, author, and publisher. However, when ten public documents are selected at random, the likelihood of any two of them following the same general arrangement on the title page is purely coincidental. Deciphering the title page becomes a major problem for the researcher and at times he may assume that a policy of deliberate confusion has been followed. The result is that many students simply avoid all forms of public documents.

Some guidelines are necessary for those who contemplate using and listing public documents in their bibliographies.

It is of utmost importance that aid be sought in the library card catalog where the material is located if proper listing in the bibliography is desired. Record this information immediately on a bibliography note card. To procrastinate will cost valuable time and increase the chance of error later. The library card catalog will give both the correct name and proper order of the author. (See the examples following these guidelines). This information is important since it is the means by which the reader may consult the work cited. If you find difficulty in locating a public document in the library card catalog, or need help in locating the library "shelf-list" catalog, ask a librarian. The shelf-list catalog lists all materials in the library in the order in which they appear on the shelf, i.e., by classification number. The information on this card should be the same as that on the author card of the library card catalog. Either the shelf-list catalog or the author card in the library card catalog will give one essentially the same information.

Another source similar to the card catalog, containing additional information on how to list documents is the National Union Catalog. Seek the help of a librarian when consulting this set.

When citing a source in the bibliography, it is better to err on the side of giving too much information than too little. The "Special Note," mentioned previously in the eight basic divisions of a bibliographic entry, provides space for additional information of this nature.

Few libraries catalog public documents under the names of personal authors appearing on the title page. However, give the first (if more than one) personal author's name appearing on the title page in the "Special Note."

Sometimes a work bears the name and title of an official, e.g. John W. Gardner, Secretary, or it may bear a title only, e.g., State

Entomologist. In either case neither the name, or title (State Entomologist), is usually referred to in the bibliographic entry. Many librarians have the habit of underscoring the first letter or two of the author (on the title page). The material will be found listed under it in the library card catalog. Therefore, cite these publications under the name of the sponsoring agency. This will greatly facilitate the reader locating the source in a library.

The author of most public documents is a corporate body. A corporate body is a group of persons or organizations identified by a name, i.e., associations, governments, business firms, institutions, conferences, committees, and specific agencies of governments.

Subordinate and related bodies to U. S. or state governments can be clarified by consulting either the United States Government Organization Manual or a specific state legislative manual.

The following examples illustrate the information found on typical cards in a library card catalog. Each is followed by an entry as it would appear in the bibliography and a sample citation note. The citation note assumes that the author has been mentioned within the text. Only the essential information is listed in the entry.

HC
110
A9
S9
1969

Symposium on Automation and Society, ***1st, University of Georgia, 1969.***
Automation and society. Edited by Ellis L. Scott and Roger W. Bolz. Athens, Ga., Center for the Study of Automation and Society [1969]

vii, 208 p. illus., ports. 22 cm.

Sponsored by the University of Georgia and the Reliance Electric Company.
Includes bibliographies.

1. Automation—Economic aspects—U. S.—Congresses. 2. Automation—Social aspects—U. S.—Congresses. I. Scott, Ellis Laverne, 1915– ed. II. Bolz, Roger William, ed. III. Georgia. University. IV. Reliance Electric Company. V. Title.

HC110.A9S9 1969 301.2′4 70—100053
MARC

Library of Congress 70 [71f30]

Symposium on Automation and Society, 1st, University, of Georgia, 1969.
[1969] Automation and Society, ed. by Ellis L. Scott and Roger W. Bolz, Center for the Study of Automation and Society, Athens, Ga.

Citation note: (1969, 58) or if author is not given in the text (Symposium on Automation . . ., 1969, 58)

RC 201 A1 W58 1962

World Forum on Syphilis and Other Treponematoses, *Washington, D. C., 1962.*

Proceedings. Atlanta, U. S. Dept. of Health, Education, and Welfare, Public Health Service, Communicable Disease Center, Venereal Disease Branch; [for sale by the Superintendent of Documents, U. S. Govt. Print. Off., 1964]

x, 521 p. illus., maps. 27 cm. (Public Health Service publication no. 997)

"Sponsors: American Social Health Association, American Venereal Disease Association [and] U. S. Department of Health, Education, and Welfare, Public Health Service. Participating agencies: World Health Organization, International Union Against the Venereal Diseases and the Treponematoses."

(Continued on next card)

64—61299

[65q4]

World Forum on Syphilis and Other Treponematoses, Washington, D. C., 1962.
[1964] Proceedings, (for sale by: U.S. Govt. Print. Off., Wash., D. C.)

Citation note: (1964, 321) or if author is not given in the text (World Forum on Syphilis . . ., 1964, 321)

HV 5800 S88 1968

Symposium on Abuse of Central Stimulants, *Stockholm, 1968.*

Abuse of central stimulants. Symposium arranged by the Swedish Committee on International Health Relations, Stockholm, November 25–27, 1968. Edited by Folke Sjöqvist and Malcolm Tottie. Stockholm, Almqvist & Wiksell, 1969.

536 p. illus. 22 cm. 34.00 S 69-30/31

Includes bibliographies.

1. Drug abuse—Congresses. 2. Stimulants—Congresses. I. Sjöqvist, Folke, ed. II. Tottie, Malcolm, ed. III. Sweden. Nämnden för internationella hälsovårdsärenden. IV. Title.

[DNLM: 1. Analeptics—congresses. 2. Drug Abuse—congresses. QV 100 S989a 1968]

HV5800.S88 1968 613.8'4 78-361663

MARC

Shared Cataloging with Library of Congress DNLM 69 [2]

Symposium on Abuse of Central Stimulants, Stockholm, 1968.
1969. Abuse of Central Stimulants, ed. by Folke Sjoqvist and Malcolm Tottie, Almqvist & Wiksell, Stockholm, Sweden.

Citation note: (1969, 127) or if author is not given in the text (Symposium on Abuse. . ., 1969, 127)

KF
26.5
N8
1971

U. S. Congress. Senate. Select Committee on Nutrition and Human Needs.
Nutrition and human needs—1971. Hearings, Ninety-second Congress, first session ... Washington, U. S. Govt. Print. Off., 1971.

pts. in v. illus. 23 cm. $2.25 (v. 1) varies.

Hearings held Feb. 23- 1971 in various cities.
Each part has also special subtitle.
Supt. of Docs. no.: Y 4.N95: N95/971

1. Nutrition. 2. Food relief—U. S. 3. School children—Food—U. S. I. Title.

KF26.5.N8 1971 641.1 70-613918
rev MARC

Library of Congress 71 [r72e3]

U. S. Congress. Senate. Select Committee on Nutrition and Human Needs.
1971. Nutrition and Human Needs--1971 (Hearings, 92d. Congress, Ist ses.) U. S. Govt. Print. Off., Wash., D.C.

Citation note: (1971, 13) or if author is not given in the text (U.S. Congress S., 1971, 13)

HS
2330
K63
A55

U. S. *Congress. House. Committee on Un-American Activities.*
Activities of Ku Klux Klan organizations in the United States. Hearings, Eighty-ninth Congress, first session. Washington, U. S. Govt. Print. Off., 1966–

v. illus., maps. 24 cm. 1.25 (v. 1) varies

Hearings held Oct. 19, 1965.

1. Ku Klux Klan (1915-) I. Title.

HS2330.K63A55 67-61542

Library of Congress [3]

U. S. Congress. House. Committee on Un-American Activities.
1966—. Activities of Ku Klux Klan Organizations in the United States (Hearings, 89th Congress, 1st ses.) Vol. 1, U. S. Govt. Print. Off., Wash., D.C.

Citation note: (1966, 25) or if author is not given in the text (U. S. Congress H., 25)

F
576 W816 **Wisconsin. State historical society.**
Collections of the State historical society of Wisconsin, edited by Lyman Copeland Draper ... being a page-for-page reprint of the original issue of 1855- v. I- Madison, The Society, 1903-

v. fronts. (ports.) plates, map, facsim. 23 cm.

Vol. I includes a "reprint of the original issue of 1855, with the addition of a memoir of Dr. Draper, and the early records of the society (1849-1854)." "Bibliography of Lyman C. Draper": v. 1, p. xxvii-xxix. Editors: 1903- R. G. Thwaites.

1. Wisconsin—Hist.—Societies, etc. I. Draper, Lyman Copeland, 1815-1891, ed. II. Thwaites, Reuben Gold, 1853-1913, ed. III. Title.

F576.W816 6—27688

Library of Congress [a64r32e½]

Wisconsin. State Historical Society.
1903— Collections of the State Historical Society of Wisconsin, ed. by Lyman Copeland Draper, Vol. 3, The Society, Madison, Wis.

Citation note: (1903, 8) or if author is not given in the text (Wis. State Hist. Soc., 1903, 8)

Radio and Television Programs

The order of the entry is as follows:

1. Narrator, person speaking, etc.
2. Date
3. Title of program
4. Special note includes program series if other than title of program, participants, etc.
5. Components—time and time zone
6. Both network and local station if possible

Radio:

Marshall, Douglas G.
1968, Ma. 16. College of the Air (discusses the university of 1990) 11 a.m., Central Time, WHA, Madison, Wis.

Citation note: (Marshall, 1968)

Television:

1968, Ma. 16. NBC News Special (a study of the balance of nature) 6:60 p.m., Central Time, NBC, N. Y.

Citation note: (1968) Mention NBC News Special in text.
1968, Ma. 16. Song of Norway (operetta about life of Edvard Grieg) 9 p.m., Central Time, WHA, Madison, Wis.

Citation note: (1968) Mention the operetta by name in text.

Records:

The information for the entry of records is taken from the record itself, plus the record holder if needed. Include the specific record number in the special note. Each entry is followed by a sample citation note.

Poe, Edgar Allan

1968. "The Masque of the Red Death," Edgar Allan Poe Tales, read by Hurd Hatfield (Record: SA-992) Spoken Arts, New Rochelle, N. Y.

Citation note: (Poe, 1968, side 1)

Date was taken from another source.

Literary Records
Classic Poems
of
SUSPENSE &
HORROR
LR 6003
23 09
SIDE II
33⅓ RPM
1 The Highwayman by Alfred Noyes
2. The Raven by Edgar Allen Poe
3. Bells by Edgar Allen Poe
MARVIN MILLER
Audio Book Co.
Los Angeles, California

Noyes, Alfred
n.d. "The Highwayman," Classic Poems of Suspense and Horror, read by Marvin Miller (Record: LR-6003) Audio Book, Los Angeles, Calif.

Citation note: (Noyes, n.d. side 1)

Clemens, Samuel Langhorne

n.d. Mark Twain Tonight, read by Hal Holbrook (Highlights from the CBS Television Network Special, Record: OL-6680) Columbia Records, N.Y., N.Y.

Citation note: (Clemens, n.d., side 1)

Real name of Mark Twain was taken from another source.

Scriptural References

Abbreviate the names of the books of the Bible and versions of the Bible. The word "Bible" and the names of the books are not underlined. The order of recording the references to the Bible in the citation note is: Name of book, chapter, verse, and version used.

(II Pe. 2:4-6, K. J.) for King James
(Mat. 13:1-4, R. S. V.) for Revised Standard
(Ro. 10:1, Jer. B.) for Jerusalem Bible
(Mk. 10:9, D. V.) for Douay Version

The same manner of referral is made to non-Christian sacred scriptures.

Example: When a verse is used within the text:

. . . "Be ye therefor perfect, even as your Father which is in heaven is perfect."[1] . . .

[1](Mat. 5:48, K. J.)

In the above case the typical citation note form is not followed because all information needed is given in the citation note. There is no need to refer to the bibliography in this case

Bible entries in the bibliography are by the title of the version:

1901. American Revised Version, N. J. Nelson.

1958. The New Testament in Modern English, tr. by J. B. Phillips, Macmillan, N. Y.

Tapes:

The information for the entry is taken from the tape storage box or reel. Include the box number in the special note.

TREASURY OF WILLIAM WORDSWORTH • SA-T-860

Wordsworth, William

n.d. Treasury of William Wordsworth (read by Robert Speaight, tape: SA-T-860) Spoken Arts, New Rochelle, N.Y.

Citation note: (Wordsworth, n.d., side one)

Leakey, Louis

n.d. Louis Leakey: Anthropologist (discusses his East African digs, tape: 19989) the Center for Cassette Studies, N. Hollywood, Calif.

Citation note: (Leakey, n.d., side 2)

Full name of publisher, place, and date may have to be obtained from another source—ask the librarian.

Miscellaneous

Chapter in a book which is part of a set having separate titles for each volume and an over-all title.

Simpson, George G.

1960. "The History of Life," The Evolution of Life (Evolution After Darwin, ed. by Sol Tax, 3 vols.) Vol. 1, U. of Chicago, Chicago, Ill.

Citation note: (Simpson, 1960, 321)

Edited by:

Commager, Henry Steele, ed.

1963. Documents of American History, 7th ed., Appleton, N. Y.

Citation note: (Commager, 1963)

Edited by and series:

Heyel, Carl, ed.

1963. The Encyclopedia of Management (Reinhold Management Reference Series) Reinhold, N. Y.

Citation note: (Heyel, 1963, 63)

Editors—three or more:

Butterfield, L. M. and others, eds.

1961. Diary and Autobiography of Adams, Vol. 4, Belknap Cambridge, Mass.

Citation note: (Butterfield, 1961, 101)

Interview:

Smith, John.

1964, D. 3. Personal Interview, New York, N. Y.

Citation note: (Smith, 1964)

Letter:

Johnson, Lewis R.

1966, Jl. 1. Personal Letter, Chicago, Ill.

Citation note: (Johnson, 1966)

Newspaper without an author:

1936, Ap. 10. "Politics of Freedom," The Cleveland Plain Dealer.

Citation note: (1936) In this case mention title of newspaper in text.

No publisher but available from:

Israel Program for Scientific Translations.

1966. Selected Bibliography of Israel Educational Materials, Vol. 1, no. 2, n.p. (available from: U. S. Dept. of Commerce, Springfield, Vir.)

Citation note: (1966) or (Israel Program for Sci. Tr., 1966)

The citation note assumes that the author was mentioned in text.

Part of a book—the author of an essay different from the editor of the book.

Brown, Bob C.

1943. "The Way Out," A Collection of Essays, ed. by Sheppard P. Hines, 2d. ed., Harper, N. Y.

Citation note: (Brown, 1943, 36)

Periodical:

Aigner, D. J.

1967, Mr. "On the Determinants of Income Equality," American Economic Review, Vol. 57, no. 1.

Citation note: (Aigner, 1967, 14)

Periodical with two authors:

Boyet, W. E. and Tolley, G. S.

1966, N. "Recreation Projection Based on Demand Analysis," Journal of Farm Economics, Vol. 48, no. 4, pt. 1.

Citation note: (Boyet, 1966, 38)

Preface:

Hart, James D.

1965. "Preface," The Oxford Companion to American Literature, 4th ed., Oxford U., N. Y.

Citation note: (Hart, 1965, iii)

Privately printed:

Barrow, Edward J.

1967. A History of Bibliography (privately printed) Edward Barrow, 12 West 9th St., Chicago, Ill.

Citation note: (Barrow, 1967)

Separate title by author in complete works edited by another with a general title:

Austen, Jane.

1932. Pride and Prejudice (The Novels of Jane Austen, ed. by R. W. Chapmen, 5 vols.) Vol. 2, 3d ed., Oxford U., N. Y.

Citation note: (Austen, 1932, 143)

(The publisher and place may be excluded from the special note when identical to that of the individual volume cited.)

Separate title for each volume with a general title by the same author:

Churchill, Winston S.

1950. The Grand Alliance (The Second World War, 6 vols.) Vol. 3, Houghton, Boston, Mass.

Citation note: (Churchill, 1950, 43-44)

Separate titles and editors of each volume in a work with a general title and editor:

Latane, J. H., ed.

1905. America as a World Power (The American Nation, ed. by A. B. Hart, 28 vols.) Vol. 25, Harper, N. Y.

Citation note: (Latane, 1905)

Series:

Hirschman, Albert O.

1958. The Strategy of Economic Development (Yale Studies in Economics) No. 10, Yale U., New Haven, Conn.

Citation note: (Hirschman, 1958, 18)

Source cited in another work but incompletely given:

Roosevelt, Theodore.

1907, 0. 3. "The Conservation of Natural Resources," The Works of Theodore Roosevelt (cited in: Henry Steele Commager, ed., 1963. Documents of American History, 7th ed., Appleton, N. Y., p. 234) Vol. 2, n.p. cited by Commager.

Citation note: (Roosevelt, 1907)

Translated and edited by other than author:

Bastiat, Frederic.

1964. Selected Essays on Political Economy, tr. by Seymour Cain, ed. by George B. de Huszar, Van Nostrand, Princeton, N. J.

Citation note: (Bastiat, 1964, 401)

Unpublished manuscript:

Hall, Fred P.

1957. Poems of Freedom (unpublished manuscript) Buffalo, N. Y.

Citation note: (Hall, 1957, 9)

INDEX

Usually an index is not necessary and is only advisable if the paper is lengthy and can thus be made more useful to the reader. A half-title page with the word "INDEX" precedes the Index text. The first page of the index text is headed:

Index (7-10 spaces from top of page)

←——————(3 spaces)

——Text——

Alphabetize and set up items in double columns. Single-space items with a double-space before the next initial letter. Indent two spaces when item is carried to the second line—also for sub-items.

Item . . . .
carry-over . . . .
carry-over . . . .
sub-items

A comma follows all items, then page number(s).

Half-title, 20
Headings
Of divisions, 33, 36
Of tables, 38-40

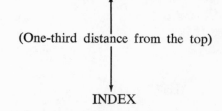

(One-third distance from the top)

INDEX

(This half-title page precedes the index text, but it is not needed for brief papers.)

(Number this page centered at the bottom)

220

1¼″

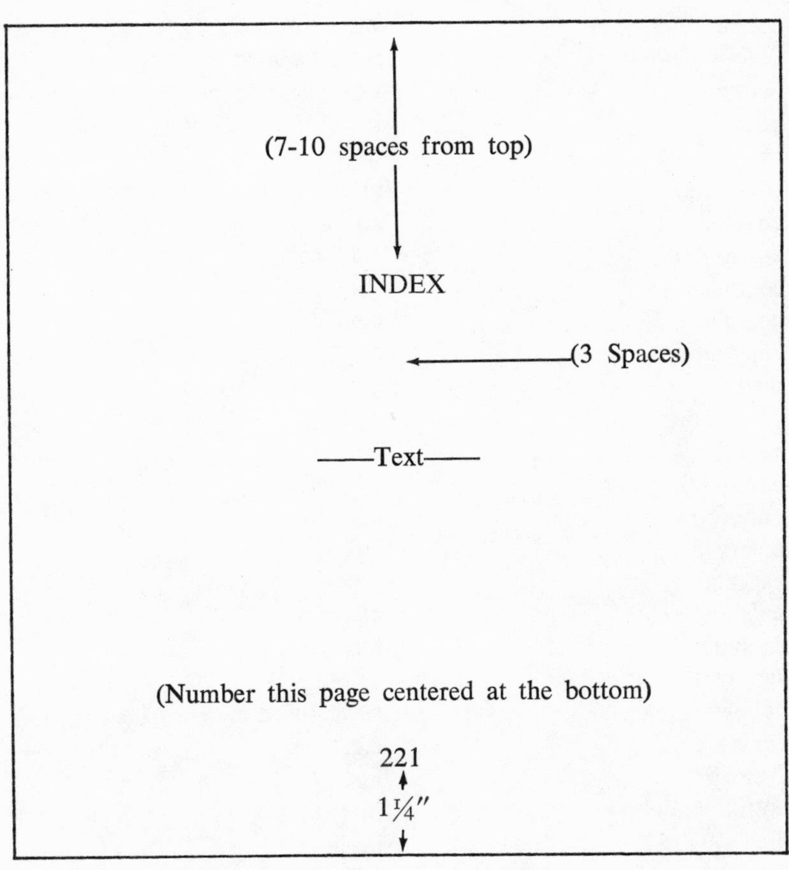

APPENDIX I

Abreviations

about	ca. (used with approximate dates, e.g., ca. 1514)
and so forth	etc. (avoid using)
anno Domini	A.D. (in the year of the Lord, precedes numerals)
anonymous	anon.
article(s)	art., arts.

before	ante
Before Christ	B.C. (follows numerals)
book(s)	bk., bks.
born	b.
bulletin	bul.
chapter(s)	ch., chs. (or chap., chaps.)
circular	cir.
column(s)	col., cols.
compiled	comp.
compiler	comp.
copyright	c.
died	d.
dissertation	diss.
edited	ed.
edition(s)	ed., eds.
editor(s)	ed., eds.
enlarged	enl.
especially	esp.
example(s)	ex., exs.
facsimile	fac.
figure(s)	fig., figs.
following page(s)	f., ff. (used after a page number)
for example	e.g.
history	hist.
introduction	introd.
line(s)	l., ll.
manuscript(s)	MS., MSS.
namely	viz.
no author	n.a.
no publisher and/or place	n.p.
no publication date	n.d.
note(s)	n., nn.
number	no.
opera	op.
page(s)	p., pp.
part(s)	pt., pts.
plate(s)	pl., pls.
preface	pref.
pseudonym	pseud.
publish, ed., -ication(s)	pub.
report	rep.

review	rev.
reviewed	rev.
revised	rev.
scene	sc.
section	sec.
second	d.
series	ser.
session	ses.
stanza	st.
supplement	suppl.
that is	i.e.
thus, so	sic. (placed in square brackets within a quotation after an obvious error)
translator, ion, ed	tr.
verse(s)	v., vs.
versus (against)	v. or vs.
volume(s)	vol., vols.

Months

Ja.—January	Jl.—July
F.—February	Ag.—August
Mr.—March	S.—September
Ap.—April	O.—October
My.—May	N.—November
Je.—June	D.—December

APPENDIX II

The sample bibliography below is arranged alphabetically by author and then by date. The nonauthor listing follows immediately after the author list, separated only by a two-inch line.

Bibliography I

Argner, D. J. and Heins, A. J.
1967, Mr. "On the Determinants of Income Equality," American Economic Review, Vol. 57, no. 1., pp. 23-31.

Anderson, Ben.

1966, Jl. 11. Personal Interview (American Library Association Convention) N. Y., N. Y.

Austen, Jane.

1932. Pride and Prejudice (The Novels of Jane Austen, ed. by R. W. Chapman, 5 vols.) Vol. 3, 3rd ed., Oxford U., N. Y., N. Y., 231 pp.

Bastiat, Frederic.

1964. Selected Essays on Political Economy, tr. by Seymour Cain, ed. by George B. de Huszar, Van Nostrand, Princeton, N. J., 335 pp.

Churchill, Winston S.

1950. The Grand Alliance (The Second World War, 6 vols.) Vol. 3, Houghton, Boston, Mass., 432 pp.

Clagett v. Daly.

1966. Supreme Court Reporter, Vol. 87, 311.

Clemens, Samuel Langhorne (Mark Twain, pseud.)

1938. The Adventures of Tom Sawyer, Harper, N. Y., N. Y., 475 pp.

Doyle, Lauren B.

1961. O. "Semantic Road Maps For Literature Searchers," Journal of the Association for Computing Machinery (cited in: Becker, Joseph. 1963. Information Storage and Retrival, Wiley, N. Y., p. 251) Vol. 8, no. 4, pp. 553-578.

Hart, James D.

1965. "Preface," The Oxford Companion to American Literature, 4th ed., Oxford U., N. Y., N. Y., 601 pp.

1965a. "New Perspectives in Literature," College English Perspectives, ed. by John B. Smith, Harper, N. Y., N. Y., pp. 91-107.

Hunt, Paul S.

1926. Knowledge of the U. S., 2d. ed., Harper, N. Y., N. Y., 198 pp.

The 3rd. ed. was not available in libraries in this area.

Johnson, Lewis E.

1966, Jl. 2. Personal Letter, Chicago, Ill., 3 pp.

Lincoln, Abraham.

1863, Jl. 6. "Letter to Henry W. Halleck," The Collected Works of Abraham Lincoln, ed. by Roy P. Basler, Vol. 6, Rutgers U., New Brunswick, N. J., 563 pp.

Pickrel, Paul, reviewer.

1967. S. "All the Little Live Things," Harpers Magazine (by Wallace Stegner) Vol. 235, no. 1408, p. 49.

Reviewer.

1968, Ja. "A Critical Approach to Children's Literature," Choice (author: James Steele Smith) Vol. 4, no. 11, p. 7.

Schreiber, Morris.

1960. Understanding and Appreciation of Poetry (record: F19120A) Side 1, Folkways Records, N. Y., N. Y.

Smith, Paul.

1963. Documents of Peace, n.p. (available from: Chautauqua County Court House, Dayton, Ohio) 39 pp.

Smith, Web. S.

n.d. The American College, Singer, Kan., 43 pp.

Twain, Mark SEE Clemens, Samuel Langhorne

U. S. Congress. House. Committee on Agriculture.

1965. General Farm Legislation (Hearing, 89th Congress, 1st ses.) U. S. Govt. Print. Off. Wash., 103 pp.

1901. American Revised Version, Nelson, N. J., 432 pp.

1909. The Koran, tr. by J. M. Rodwell (Everyman's Library) Dutton, N. Y., N. Y., 401 pp.

1963. Shakespeare's Theatre (Tape TE9026) Educational Audio Visual, Pleasantville, N. Y.

1966. "Trebmius, Gaires," Encyclopaedia Britannica, Vol. 22, Encyclopaedia Britannica, Chicago, Ill., p. 346.

1966a. McGraw-Hill Encyclopedia of Science and Technology, Vol. 13, McGraw-Hill, N. Y., N. Y.

1966, Ag. 10. "Politics of Freedom," The Cleveland Plain Dealer.

Note in the entries listed above:

a. Each entry is listed alphabetically by author.
b. When two or more entries are by the same author, the author is only listed for the first entry. The entry having the earliest date is listed first. If the years are the same, they are differentiated by adding an "a" or "b" to the date, i.e., 1966, 1966a, 1966b, etc. This is for the purpose of citing the specific bibliographic entry from the text.
c. A two-inch line separates the author from the nonauthor list.

Bibliography II

BOOKS

PRIMARY SOURCES:

Churchill, Winston S.

1950. The Grand Alliance (The Second World War, 6 vols.) Vol. 3, Houghton, Boston, Mass.

Hall, Fred P.

1957. Poems of Freedom (unpublished manuscript) Buffalo, N. Y.

SECONDARY SOURCES:

Green, Richard A.

1926. "Thoughts on Andrew Johnson," Essays on Green, comp. by Paul Owen, Lake Mich.

Hunt, Paul S.

1937. The Writings of Thomas Mann, 2d. ed., Harper, N. Y. N. Y.

The third ed. was not available in libraries in this area.

PERIODICALS

Boyet, W. E. and Tolley, G. S.

1966. N. "Recreation Projection Based on Demand Analysis," Journal of Farm Economics, Vol. 48, no. 4, pt. 1.

Pickrel, Paul, reviewer.

1967. S. "All the Little Live Things," Harpers Magazine (by Wallace Stegner) Vol. 235. no. 1408.

NON-BOOK MATERIALS

Scheiber, Morris.

1960. Understanding and Appreciation of Poetry (record: F19120A) Side 1, Folkways Record, N. Y.

Index

INDEX